C000187021

Legendary
DARTMOOR

PUBS & INNS

EXPLORE IN THE FOOTSTEPS OF SHERLOCK HOLMES
& THE HOUND OF THE BASKERVILLES

Simon Butler

HALSGROVE

PUBLISHED IN ASSOCIATION WITH THE DARTMOOR TRUST ARCHIVE

First published in Great Britain in 2016

Text © 2016 Simon Butler
Historic photos from the Halsgrove Archive and
the Dartmoor Archive

A CIP catalogue record for this book is available
from the British Library.

ISBN 978 0 85710 106 8

PiXZ Books
Halsgrove House, Ryelands Business Park,
Bagley Road, Wellington, Somerset TA21 9PZ
Tel: 01823 653777
Fax: 01823 216796
email: sales@halsgrove.com

An imprint of Halstar Ltd, part of the
Halsgrove group of companies
Information on all Halsgrove titles is
available at: www.halsgrove.com

Printed and bound in China by
Everbest Printing Investment Ltd

For Sonny

*Frontispiece: Landlord John Butler and daughter
outside the Sun Inn, Ashburton c.1900.*

CONTENTS

DARTMOOR

LOCATION OF PRINCIPAL PLACES APPEARING IN THE BOOK

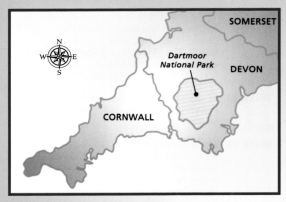

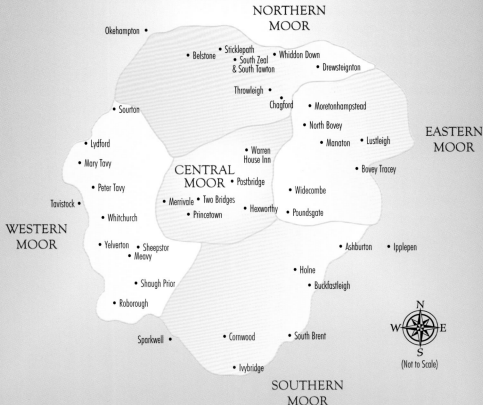

4

FOREWORD

Those of us who know Dartmoor well can still find places that provide the sense of wildness and solitude that Sir Arthur Conan Doyle experienced on his visit in 1901, and which he used to such good effect in *The Hound of the Baskervilles*. However, as our population increases and the popularity of recreational pursuits grow, so our National Parks will come under increasing pressure and it will become a much rarer thing to *'walk all day and never see one human being'*, as Doyle described the moor.

Along with the work of the National Park Authority there are many smaller organisations and groups that dedicate their time to ensuring that Dartmoor remains a place in which the natural landscape, the lives of those who live here and those who visit, achieve a harmony in which the essential nature of the environment is conserved.

The Dartmoor Trust is one such body, a charity that provides support for local projects and whose members appreciate and care about Dartmoor. But in order to best care for the future we most also look to the past, and the Dartmoor Trust Archive, from which many of the photographs in this book are drawn, provides this vital link to our history.

It is an archive open to all. I encourage you to explore the archive online, to add further information to existing images, or to provide photographs of your own. Should you wish to be involved I invite you to contact us – Dartmoor's future is in our hands.

Lt Col. (Retired) Tony Clark OBE
Chairman
The Dartmoor Trust & Archive

THE DARTMOOR TRUST ARCHIVE

Archiving photographs is important for they show us how things change. Here is the Duchy Hotel, Princetown, seen c.1900, in the 1920s and how it looks today.

T he publication of this book celebrates, in part, the 20th anniversary of the establishment of the Dartmoor Trust, a milestone worthy of note for without that organisation there would be no Dartmoor Trust Archive. The Trust itself came about through the foresight of the Dartmoor National Park Authority which, in 1996, saw the advantages of an independent charitable body that, whilst championing the overall aims of the Authority, could undertake projects that were outside the statutory body's remit.

In those two decades the Dartmoor Trust, under the guidance of its Trustees, has provided financial support to a wide range of organisations and individuals, from the restoration ancient artefacts to major educational exhibitions.

From the outset the Trustees determined to look for a keystone project that would underpin the overall objectives of the Trust, establishing a permanent profile alongside its continuing support for local initiatives. Having explored the possibility of a physical archive, the Trustees settled on a purely digital archive – largely photographic – dedicated to collecting and preserving important images of Dartmoor.

Restoration of the broken shaft of the ancient Shaden Cross with funding from The Dartmoor Trust.

Initially exploring links to existing archives, the Trustees recognised that the rapid development of the worldwide web would make it possible to set up its own on-line archive to which it could add images and related information as they became available. This became the basis of the Dartmoor Trust Archive as it exists today – a sophisticated data platform providing easy public access to over 20 000 images.

Such successes are not achieved without dedication and effort behind the scenes, and alongside their work on other projects the Trustees found themselves engaged in promoting the archive to encourage wider public interest. To this end, in 2000, a book *Dartmoor Century I* was published based on the late Victorian photographs of Robert Burnard. The book was launched accompanied by a major exhibition of photographs, and a year later *Dartmoor Century II* was published to celebrate the addition to the archive of 2300 photographs from the Sydney Taylor Collection. This was followed by the digitisation of the Chapman Collection of 4000 photographs, dating from the Victorian period to the 1960s. The fact that the majority of these thousands of images previously existed in negative form only, many as fragile glass plates, made it almost impossible for the public to have access to them. At last, through carefully digitising each photograph, it was possible to reveal – often for the first time for many years – thousands of unique images of Dartmoor.

Such work is not without cost, and while the Trust has been assiduous in working within constrained budgets, it has been fortunate in seeking and receiving various generous grants and donations in order to maintain and develop the archive, constantly adding new photographs and upgrading the site and data storage, as the technology develops.

In common with most charitable bodies, this era of austerity places severe constraints on finances, with the consequent need to seek further funding in order to continue the Trust's work. Among several new initiatives, the Trustees are publishing a series of books, of which this is the first, each covering a particular theme or aspect of Dartmoor based on images selected from the archive.

The bar of the Valiant Soldier pub in Ashburton, a museum founded with the help of the Dartmoor Trust.

Archiving photographs is important for they reveal to us things that have disappeared. East Street Ashburton c.1960 showing both the Golden Lion and the the Red Lion, once thriving pubs, now closed.

Archiving photographs is important for they reveal to us that some things hardly ever change. Haytor in the 1920s and today.

Sales of these books and accompanying exhibitions will certainly help raise funds but it is as promotional vehicles that they will play a most significant role, particularly at a time when the on-line presence of the archive is undergoing a major facelift.

The Trust now has an opportunity to facilitate the addition to the archive of one of the last major Dartmoor photographic collections yet to be digitised. Working with the Torquay Natural History Museum, the Dartmoor Trust is embarking upon the digitisation of the photographic collection of R. Hansford Worth (1868–1950), antiquarian, historian and author, whose monumental work, *Worth's Dartmoor*, published in 1953, remains a classic of Dartmoor literature.

The collection totals over 7000 images, largely film negatives and glass plates, the former being unique insofar as they are contained in individual wallets with each negative described as to location, date and other details. The photographs range in date from the 1880s through to the 1940s.

There is no doubt that this collection remains the most comprehensive single body of images of Dartmoor as yet largely unseen. Making this collection available for the enjoyment and education of the public would significantly increase our overall knowledge of the moor and constitute a major contribution to the Dartmoor Archive.

To discover more about the work of the Dartmoor Trust visit www.dartmoortrust.org and the Dartmoor Trust Archive at www.dartmoorarchive.org.

PREFACE

Friends will say my main qualification for writing about the inns of Dartmoor is that I have frequented most of them. In younger days, village cricket matches always ended at a pub – usually followed by a meandering trip homewards via various other favourite haunts – always with a designated driver naturally.

Few counties match Devon for its variety of country pubs, and yet we are losing them more rapidly than ever in recent years due to drink driving laws (a good thing), the smoking ban (ditto) and the fact that a pint or two, that used to be part of a countryman's working day, is now unaffordable by many. As 'regulars' declined so publicans and breweries had to find new ways of attracting custom. Few pubs survive today without serving food and many provide fare of such a high standard that bar trade has become insignificant or else has disappeared. This is all to the good, but it's seldom a bad thing to acknowledge the passing of 'how things used to be' without a little regret.

Old Dartmoor Inn sign, Merrivale

Dartmoor is home to one of the world's most enduring stories, Arthur Conan Doyle's *The Hound of the Baskervilles*. This book is intended to point readers in the direction of a selection of Dartmoor pubs and inns which themselves have a direct association with the author and the legend of *The Hound*, or have their own legendary connections – often both. This is not a pub guide describing the quality of food, or the disposition of the publican. It's a personal selection that on a typically dismal Dartmoor day may lead you – as it has me – to a cheering drink by a warm fireside, or when the weather's fine, to encourage the reader to explore a little farther afield where Dartmoor legends abound.

The East Dart, Postbridge

Directions to the pubs themselves should be easy enough to find by visiting the pubs' own websites. Sat nav is fine but postcodes on the moor often cover more than one address so at least look at a map before staring out, unless you already know where you're going.

It would be tempting simply to suggest that you stop and ask a local for directions – at some peril. At the risk of stereotyping here's a warning anecdote:

'I say, can you tell me how to get to North BOWVEY?'
'How do 'ee get to North Bovey? Well 'ee goes along this yer road a guidish way and you come to dree vorks in the roads. Well [with much waving of arms], *you don't take no notice of 'ee, and you don't take no notice of 'ee, but you go along 'ee until you comes to two thatched cottages. Don'ee take no notice o' they, but go on till you comes to vower crossroads. Don' take no notice of dree o' they but go straight on a guidish bit further than you think you'm gwain, and then... where was it you said you was gwain?'*

The place where legends are born. Arthur Conan Doyle stayed at the Duchy Hotel Princetown in 1901 and it was here that the story of The Hound of the Baskervilles *was fleshed out. Here the hotel is seen around the time of Doyle's visit, with the proprietor Aaron Rowe and staff standing at the door.*

Ending of course with the time-honoured, '...well, I wouldn't have started from here.'

British pubs are disappearing at an alarming rate, around 20 000 have closed in the past three decades, and many that once seemed impervious to change on Dartmoor have closed their doors for the last time. Of those that remain, one is only too aware of how fragile is their continuing existence. Let's hope their names don't all become the stuff of legend.

Simon Butler
Dartmoor 2016

INTRODUCTION

Sir Arthur Conan Doyle was no stranger to the Westcountry. His most famous creation, Sherlock Holmes, and his greatest adventure, *The Hound of the Baskervilles,* was originally serialised in *The Strand Magazine* from August 1901 to April 1902. Inspiration for the story came from a friend, Bertram Fletcher Robinson, and was based partly on the legend of Richard Cabell, a cursed Devon country squire, and of a hellish hound. Cabell's tomb can be visited in Buckfastleigh on the edge of Dartmoor. The story has continued to hold enormous fascination through films and most recently in Benedict Cumberbatch's TV portrayal of the world's greatest detective.

Arthur Conan Doyle (1859-1930)

Born in Edinburgh in 1859, Doyle later trained in that city in medicine before working as a medical assistant in Birmingham. In 1880 he embarked upon a whaling ship, the *Hope,* bound for the Arctic Ocean – an adventure in which he nearly lost his life – before completing his studies the following year, after which he found work as ship's surgeon on board a steamer heading for the West African coast, narrowly escaping with his life after contracting typhoid.

In 1882 Doyle joined George Turnavine Budd's practice in Stonehouse near Plymouth in Devon and so began his association with the Westcountry. In that year Doyle travelled out to the edge of Dartmoor, an excursion that inspired him to write an article, *Dry Plates on a Wet Moor,*

On his excursion from Stonehouse to Roborough in 1881 Doyle would have passed close to the aptly named Dartmoor Hotel which stood on the Tavistock Road out of Plymouth. Twenty years later his most famous story would be published.

The Baskerville horse bus which travelled between Plymouth and Roborough. Fletcher Robinson gave Harry Baskerville a copy of The Hound inscribed 'with apologies for using the name'.

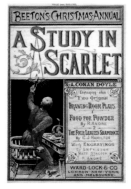

The world is introduced to Sherlock Holmes in Beeton's Christmas Annual, *1887.*

for the *British Journal of Photography*. The 'moor' he visited was a bleak area around the village of Roborough (on his way to Tavistock) where he frequented an equally inhospitable establishment he calls the Admiral Vernon which we know today, more happily, as The Lopes Arms. It has been suggested that he may also have made his first encounter with a name which was to become forever associated with him, for the Plymouth to Roborough horse bus was operated by the Baskerville family.

Shortly after this date Doyle dissolved his partnership with Budd and travelled to Portsmouth where he set up his own medical practice; for eight years living happily in Southsea, marrying Louise Hawkins in 1885. A year later he wrote *A Study in Scarlet*, published in 1887, in which he introduces Sherlock Holmes, the world's most famous detective.

Three years later came the second Holmesian story, *A Sign of Four*, published in the Philadelphia-based magazine *Lippincott's*, and in 1891 Doyle and his family moved to London.

The Lopes Arms in Roborough is the building hidden by the horse bus, photographed here in the early years of the twentieth century. Doyle stayed at the inn in 1882 on his first excursion to Dartmoor.

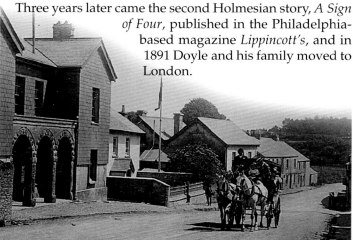

12

Here began his long association with George Newnes and *The Strand* magazine, with 24 Sherlock Holmes short stories appearing between 1891 and 1893 and a further 32 between 1901 and 1927. Doyle was now a celebrity author and travelled widely giving lecture tours, including visits to the USA. He several times visited Devon during the latter years of the nineteenth century – a period during which Louise's health deteriorated and Doyle began a liaison with Jean Leckie, fourteen years his junior, who was later to become his second wife. But it was not until 1901 that Doyle reacquainted himself with Dartmoor.

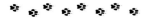

In 1900 Doyle had served in South Africa as a civilian doctor in the war again the Boers. On the boat home he struck up with a journalist, Bertram Fletcher Robinson, and the two established a lasting friendship. In later correspondence Doyle acknowledges that Robinson gave him the 'central idea' for the story of *The Hound*, and the two men certainly worked closely as the idea developed. Thus it was, in 1901, the two visited Dartmoor together, basing themselves it is said, at Robinson's parents' home, Park Hill House, in Ipplepen. Here the coachman was Henry (known as 'Harry') Baskerville and it was he who drove Doyle out on to the moor and from whom the famous fictional name was taken.

We know from Doyle's diaries and letters that the party visited many of the places on the moor that were eventually incorporated into the book, either as dramatic actual locations or as fictional placenames, often thinly disguised. Most famous of these, perhaps, is Doyle's treacherous bog the Grimpen Mire, a chilling amalgam of Fox Tor Mire and Grimspound.

Doyle's stories were serialised in The Strand Magazine *and fans queued up outside the Newnes offices when* The Hound of the Baskervilles *was published in order to be the first to read the next instalment.*

Ipplepen as it looked around the time of Doyle's journey in 1901. The Wellington Inn sign can be seen on the right.

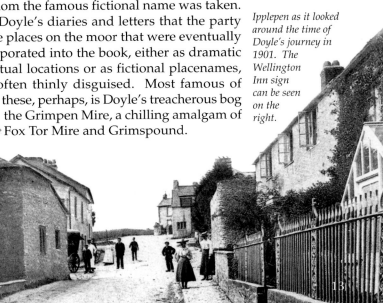

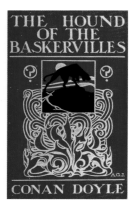

The cover of the first edition.

There has been much speculation about the precise route that Doyle and his companions took while on their moorland journey in search of 'colour' for their story. We know for a fact that the party stayed at the Duchy Hotel in Princetown as Doyle wrote to his mother from here: *'Dearest of Mams, Here I am in the highest town in England. Robinson and I are exploring the moor over our Sherlock Holmes book... We did 14 miles on the moor today...'*

In his excellent book *The Hound of the Baskervilles: Hunting the Dartmoor Legend*, Philip Weller provides many plausible locations for sites Doyle visited, interpreting the fictional placenames he used and suggesting actual locations for each.

We know that Doyle was an accomplished sportsman, playing first class cricket and taking the role of goalkeeper for the football team that was to become Portsmouth FC. His conviviality would invariably have drawn him to the local inn and there were plenty for him to chose from on and around Dartmoor at the time he visited. *White's Directory* of 1897 lists over 250 inns and public houses hereabouts.

In *The Hound of the Baskervilles*, while the Northumberland Hotel in London appears (and exists, today), there is only one Dartmoor inn referred to in the story. *"It was a pleasant walk of four miles along the edge of the moor, leading me at last to a small grey hamlet, in which two larger buildings, which proved to be the inn and the house of Dr. Mortimer, stood high above the rest."*

However, of the pubs and inns included in the present book almost all have a direct connection either to Doyle, his journeys on the moor, associated legends, or through the thirty or so feature films and many TV adaptations inspired by the original story.

Not the Hound of the Baskervilles. Thomas Hext, Landlord of the Warren House Inn in 1882 stands with his dog at the entrance to this well known Dartmoor building.

14

THE EASTERN MOOR

MANATON

Despite being one of Dartmoor's largest parishes by area, Manaton boasts only one hostelry, the Kestor Inn, which sits foursquare in the centre of the village. However, the parish itself has a rich and interesting history regarding earlier inns and the Kestor is perfectly placed at the centre of any number of interesting walks. It is also a popular stopping off point for cyclists many of whom regularly test themselves on the long climb from Bovey Tracey.

Today popular with walkers and cyclists the Kestor Inn replaced the earlier Half Moon which stood on Manaton's village green.

Built around 1910 the Kestor and nearby tearooms served early tourists to the moor who came by train to Bovey Tracey or Lustleigh and walked or took a carriage to Manaton, which in those days must have seemed quaintly remote.

Perhaps it was this lucrative new trade that persuaded its builder, James Harvey, to move from Manaton's former public house at the top of the village green, now a private dwelling, but originally the Half Moon Inn. Those looking for a pleasant short walk between the two should look out for Slinkers' Lane which takes the walker from the Kestor up to the village green avoiding traffic on the road.

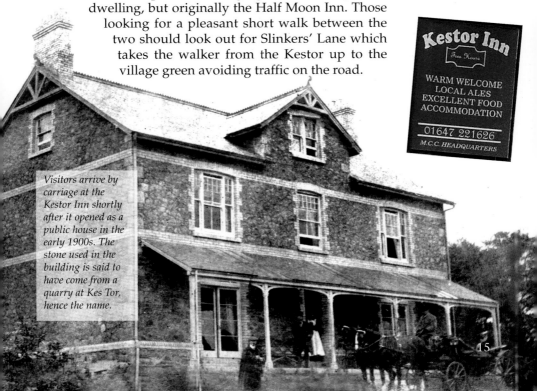

Kestor Inn
Free House

WARM WELCOME
LOCAL ALES
EXCELLENT FOOD
ACCOMMODATION

01647 221626

M.C.C. HEADQUARTERS

Visitors arrive by carriage at the Kestor Inn shortly after it opened as a public house in the early 1900s. The stone used in the building is said to have come from a quarry at Kes Tor, hence the name.

15

Opposite: The mysterious cross in Manaton churchyard, once the object of 'pagan' rituals.

The area abounds with legends and adjacent to the green stands Manaton's parish church, St Winifreds. Here in the churchyard, close to the porch, stands an old granite cross which in early Victorian times the vicar took down and had secretly buried to deny the villagers their 'pagan' practices. The story goes that during funerals the villagers carried the coffin three times around the ancient cross before burying their dead. This no longer happens despite the fact that the old cross was rediscovered and replaced!

There are various candidates for locations thought to have inspired Sir Arthur Conan Doyle in writing *The Hound of the Baskervilles*. Among these is Hound Tor, said itself to be haunted by the petrified remains of a pack of hounds, one of a number of such legends on the moor. A little distance south, also in Manaton parish, stands a tall monolith, Bowerman's nose. This too is associated with a hunter and his hounds turned to stone by witches.

Legends of black hounds and witches abound in the area. Bowerman's Nose (above) is said to be all that remains of a hunter who was turned to stone along with his hounds. Hound Tor, has been used in filming The Hound of the Baskervilles *and few places on the moor match the drama of these ramparts of stricken stone.*

Adjacent to the car park at Hound Tor, at Swallerton Gate, stands a cottage, now a private house, once known as The Hound Tor Inn, although it was probably no more than a 'Wink', as informal drinking houses were once called. In his book *High Dartmoor* Eric Hemery describes this as a cider house on the wool trading route between Ashburton and Chagford. The inn closed sometime around 1840.

Hemery records that he was personally acquainted with Bill Baskerville, nephew of Henry from whom Doyle took the name of his character, and who, as coachman drove the author and Fletcher Robinson around the moor.

The former Hound Tor Inn, now a private residence, appeared in an early film representing Merripit House in The Hound of the Baskervilles. *It is also the place where explorer Thor Heyerdhal of Kon Tiki fame wrote much of his book in the late 1940s.*

Heatree House, near to Hound Tor, was claimed to be home to members of the Baskerville family, and is suggested as inspiration for the fictional Baskerville Hall, as is Leighon, a country house settled in the valley of nearby Becka Brook.

While the Kestor Inn presents a very good reason for visiting Manaton, the inn itself is a good quarter mile from the original settlement which centred on the church of St Winifred and its adjacent green. It's a delightful location in itself and had the original inn, the Half Moon, remained it would surely be one of England's most idyllic hostelries.

The former inn, Half Moon, nestles at the head of Manaton village green. The main photo is as the inn looked in 1889, little changed today.

NORTH BOVEY

Ancient stone cross that stands on the green at North Bovey.

The yard at the Ring of Bells in 1894 from a photograph by Robert Burnard. Opposite: A reconstruction of the scene in 2015 showing remarkably little change.

Everyone's idea of a perfect Devon village. Stone-built thatched cottages surround an idyllic little village green, where the pub sign leads you down to The Ring of Bells. Sitting in the garden here on a summer evening, shadowed by fragrant lime trees with the church tower glimpsed across the green, it is indeed a kind of English perfection.

For many years the landlords here were the Brackenbury family whose namesake, Sir Robert, was Constable of the Tower of London during the reign of wicked Richard III (recently notorious for his exhumation from a council car park). It was this Brackenbury who refused to kill the Princes in the Tower, though on the orders of the king he did hand over the keys to the eventual murderers.

Some controversy surrounds the authorship of *The Hound of the Baskervilles*, with one writer at least contending it was not

18

written by Doyle at all. However, the latter does give ample credit to his friend Bertram Fletcher Robinson for sowing the seeds of the story and originally insisted that his publisher include both their names as authors.

On their journeying around the moor the two men collected local tales that might be added to give 'colour' to their proposed work, such as that related by author Lois Deacon. In her book *Dartmoor With a Difference* she describes several ghost stories associated with the North Bovey, and includes one which rings truer than most.

It involves the coachman, a Mr Coniam, employed by the Revd William Henry Thornton, rector of North Bovey from 1866 to 1916. A notorious frequenter of The Ring of Bells, Coniam staggered home one night across the unlit village green and at the churchyard steps he was confronted by a pale apparition which raised its arms and croaked, 'I've lost me graaave!'

'Lost yer grave 'ave ee?' came the drunkards response. 'Then you better go an' haunt up old Charlie Waldern, the Sexton. He'll soon find it for 'ee.'

The Ring of Bells was said to be built as accommodation for the men who built the church in the 13th century. Badly damaged by fire in 2016, the inn was temporarily closed.

The Manor House
North Bovey c.1930,
(now Bovey Castle)
was a location used
in the first talking
picture of The
Hound of the
Baskervilles, 1931.
Inset: The US poster
for the movie.

A mile or so from the village lies Bovey Castle, formerly the Manor House Hotel and before that home to the W.H. Smith, Lord Hambleden. This imposing residence has been put forward as another candidate for Baskerville Hall and indeed fits Doyle's description in his story quite neatly. However, the contention falls down on the fact the house was not built until 1906 some five years after *The Hound of the Baskervilles* was published.

The Manor House was however used in making the film, released in 1931, starring Robert Rendel as Sherlock Holmes and with a screenplay by Edgar Wallace. This was the first sound version movie ever made of the story and the first to use actual locations on Dartmoor.

LUSTLEIGH

Dating from the sixteenth century, starting life as a farm-house, The Cleave offers everything one could hope for in a Devon village pub: low-beamed ceilings and pretty windows snug beneath the thatch. Gatehouse Farm, seen in the photograph on the page opposite, became a public house in the mid 1800s though, surprisingly, an early landlord, a Mr Woodward, was 'a teetotaler who did much to promote temperance.'!

The Cleave is named after the steep gorge of the River Bovey which forms part of Lustleigh parish's western boundary. Here legend has it that a ghostly party of knights process

down the valley but, apparitions aside, certainly the steep climb to the summit is well worth the effort. At the north-western end of this massive hillside stand the visible remains of an Iron Age hillfort where a Roman coin was recently found among the scattered boulders. The view from the summit provides panoramic vistas of the eastern slopes of Dartmoor, taking in the distant shapes of Hound Tor and Haytor. To the west lies the estuary of the River Teign and the sea. Although less than a mile from Lustleigh village centre it's quite a climb so a visit to The Cleave on your return makes for a satisfying trip.

Lustleigh also has strong ties with Sherlock Holmes but, as with North Bovey, its connection rests on the movie industry and not with Doyle's earlier visits to Dartmoor. This film, shot during the winter of 1929–30, established several firsts: it was the first sound version of *The Hound of the Baskervilles*, and is the first

Lustleigh Cleave painted in 1820 by Francis Stevens.

21

Lustleigh Station transformed into Baskerville Halt for the 1930s filming of The Hound of the Baskervilles.

which can definitely be identified as being made on Dartmoor. Lustleigh's tiny station was renamed 'Baskerville Halt' for the shooting which was interrupted when snow fell on the area overnight.

The Cleave has a direct connection to all this as the bistro area at the rear of the inn was formerly the station waiting room. Hound burger anyone?

The Cleave Inn today.

MORETONHAMPSTEAD

This largely unspoilt moorland town is the eastern gateway to the moor for those travelling on the old road from Exeter. It is the closest habitation to the Manor House Hotel used in the 1931 film and is a town replete with its own legends – and pubs. At the time Doyle was touring the moor, Moreton boasted no fewer than seventeen hostelries of varying repute, the best of them serving passengers from the railway which opened here in 1866. These included both the White Hart and White Horse (now called The Horse) which stand within a few yards of each other, two of the four inns remaining today.

George Street in Moretonhamsptead c.1920 with the White Hart Hotel on the left.

23

Ford Street, Moreton c.1920 with the sign of what was then the Punch Bowl Inn seen above the cart on the right. Today the Union Inn stands a little farther along also on the right.

Superb Victorian detail on the front of the Union Inn.

As with many writers of crime fiction, in preparing his stories we know that Doyle was an avid collector of local tales from which he borrowed names and events to populate his own writings. Moreton's cause célèbre involved the murder of a local farmer, Jonathan May, in 1835, at the hands of Buckingham Joe. Found bloody and barely conscious some distance from the town, May was carried back to the White Hart where he died the following day. Buckingham Joe was later arrested along with an accomplice Edmund Galley* and both were tried and found guilty, the former hanged, the latter transported to Australia. Through its connection to the murder the White Hart continued to excite interest among its visitors for many years.

BOVEY TRACEY

Tomorrow morning I shall find my way to Coombe Tracey... a long step will have been made to clearing one incident in this chain of mysteries... I have not lived for years with Sherlock Holmes for nothing.

The sign of the Bell Inn Bovey Tracey.

So declares Dr Watson in *The Hound of the Baskervilles*, and while there is no such place as Coombe Tracey on Dartmoor, this is another example of Doyle's inventive use of local names. Indeed in his original manuscript the town is named as Newton Abbott (not 'Abbot') throughout and Doyleian

*Galley's conviction was always suspect and he was eventually granted a Parliamentary pardon. Though a free man he never returned from Australia.

scholars assume this is the probable location of the station to and from which Holmes and Watson journey in their quest to solve the mystery of *The Hound*. While Newton Abbot is the obvious location, for it served main line trains direct to the metropolis, the station at Bovey Tracey was a mere fifteen minutes by branch line and was an obvious gateway to the moor. Watson stays at a hotel at Coombe Tracey before the arrival of Holmes and its namesake, Bovey Tracey, was well served with several hostelries offering accommodation, horse and motor transport up on to the high moor. These included the Railway Hotel, the Dolphin, the Union (now the Cromwell) and the Bell, all but the first named surviving today. Sadly, the oldest of all, the Old Thatch, was recently demolished following a fire in 2008.

As with many small towns, once served by numerous hostelries, Bovey Tracey has suffered the disappearance of several public houses including the King of

Bovey Tracey station in the early years of the 20th century. Charabancs wait to take tourists on to the moor.

The Railway Hotel (left) and the Dolphin Hotel (right) took advantage of the arrival of the railway and the growth in tourism from the late Victorian period.

The Old Thatch, Bovey Tracey, lost forever.

The Cromwell, formerly the Union.

Prussia and the Riverside Inn both recent losses, while the Union has changed its name and is now the Cromwell, named after the Lord Protector who, with a contingent of his army, surprised a group of Royalist officers playing cards in the Old Thatch. It is said they escaped by throwing their table stakes from the window of the inn, thus distracting the Roundheads.

HAYTOR

Haytor's massive granite summit draws visitors to its impressive slopes throughout the year. Below the tor are the haunting ruins of vast quarries that once supplied granite for

The Rock Inn stands at the end of the row of former quarry-men's cottages.

many of London's best known buildings. Here too are the remains of the tramway, built in 1820, to convey the granite from here to the Stover Canal ten miles distant. This was the brainchild of James Templer whose son George then inherited the estate, building cottages nearby to house the quarry workers and alongside which stands the Rock Inn.

Quarries feature significantly in *The Hound of the Baskervilles* as places of mystery and foreboding while Haytor itself appears in the 1983 filming of the story starring Ian Richardson as Holmes. Legend has it that the Rock Inn is home to Belinda, the ghostly spectre of a serving woman murdered in the mid 1800s by the wife of a coachman with whom she had an affair.

Built in 1903 to satisfy the increasing tourism traffic to Dartmoor, the Moorlands Hotel stands in the shadow of Haytor. It was here that another great crime writer Agatha Christie stayed in 1916 while writing her whodunnit *The Mysterious Affair at Styles.*

Known as 'the Cathedral of the Moor' the church of Saint Pancras dominates the valley in which the village of Widecombe-in-the-Moor lies.

WIDECOMBE-IN-THE-MOOR

Famous for the story of Widecombe Fair and the song of Tom Pearce's grey mare, the tiny village of Widecombe nestles deep in a combe overlooked by rocky tors. Its principal hostelry, the Old Inn, lies at the centre of the village close to the church and provides a perfect starting (or stopping!) point for anyone wishing to explore the area.

Noted Sherlockian scholar William Stuart Baring-Gould (who wrote a 'biography' of the great detective, *Sherlock Holmes of Baker Street* published in 1962) suggests Widecombe plays the role of the village of Grimpen in *The Hound*: 'a small clump of buildings here is the hamlet of Grimpen'. This Baring-Gould (1913–67) was the nephew of the better known Revd Sabine Baring-Gould (1834–1924), antiquarian and man of letters, whose writings on Dartmoor almost certainly influenced Doyle with regard to Dartmoor. Both men wrote for the same magazines that brought Holmes to fame.

Above and right: Revd Sabine Baring-Gould stands at the entrance to Grimspound the largest of Dartmoor's prehistoric enclosures. Both he and Doyle contributed stories to the same magazines.

The Reverend was a leading light in the Dartmoor Exploration Committee that in the nineteenth century did much excavation and restoration of the prehistoric monuments that are found in great numbers on the moor – most famously perhaps at Grimspound, a late Bronze Age settlement – its name almost certainly giving rise to the fictitious Grimpen in the Baskerville story. While Grimspound lies in Manaton parish by road it lies closer to Widecombe.

The Anglo Saxons knew 'Grim' as the Devil and it is a prefix to placenames associated with evil legends throughout England. And the Devil himself paid a visit to Widecombe, as related in the following section on Poundsgate.

Historian Eric Hemery records in the 1960s meeting Bill Baskerville, then living in Widecombe, the nephew of Henry, better known as Harry Baskerville, the coachman who drove Doyle and Robinson around the moor.

The Old Inn seen around the time of Doyle's visit to Dartmoor in 1901.

The Old Inn today.

The Rugglestone Inn.

Widecombe's second inn, The intriguingly named Rugglestone, is tucked away a short walk from the village centre. While almost cottage-sized it attracts large numbers of patrons, in no small part due to its unspoilt interior, little changed since the time of Doyle's Dartmoor excursion.

The pub takes its name from a nearby tor known as Rugglestone Rock the topmost part of which was a logan or 'rocking' stone, one of a number found across the moor. These stones, often massive in size could nonetheless be rocked to and fro with seemingly little effort and were often attributed with magical powers. The Ruggle Stone was said only to move with the help of the church key – but today even with Divine assistance the stone refuses to budge.

POUNDSGATE

The postman, Walter Butlin, outside the Tavistock Inn c.1890.

This tiny community, lying to the south of Widecombe, is the source of a powerful legend associated with real and terrible events. According to the story recorded in the Tavistock Inn at Poundsgate, local card sharp Jan Reynolds (aka Bobby Read) made a pact with the Devil that if ever he should fall asleep in church, the Devil could take his soul.

The Tavistock Inn today.

One Sunday, as the gambler nodded off in Widecombe church, pack of cards in hand, the Devil arrived at the Tavistock Inn calling for a drink and demanding to know the whereabouts of his dissolute victim. The beer hissed as it went down the Devil's throat and when he put his ale pot down it left a scorch mark on the bar. Riding to Widecombe the Devil conjured up a storm and amid the thunder and lightning he claimed the soul of the gambler and three others who earlier had been playing cards in church, whisking them off to hell.

The legend is born of real events, for as one historical account has it:

On Sunday afternoon, October 21, 1638, Widecombe church was much damaged by lightning, which killed 4 and injured 62 of the congregation then assembled in divine worship. The tower was shattered extensively, and one of the large pinnacles fell through the roof of the nave, and a large beam dropped between the pulpit and reading-desk, without injuring the vicar or the clerk.

Woodcut depicting the storm of 1638 that destroyed much of Widecombe's church tower.

The Devil visits the Tavistock Inn.

31

THE CENTRAL MOOR

THE WARREN HOUSE INN

Isolated in winter, abuzz with tourists in summer, the Warren House Inn has a fascinating history. Inset, the plaque set up by John Wills marking completion of the new building in 1845.

Perhaps the quintessential moorland inn, the Warren House and its setting is perfect for the flowering of legends. At 1350 feet it is one of the highest pubs in England and its location one of the most remote, although one might not think so if visiting on a warm summer day, for the place is thronged with parked cars and walkers. Only in winter does one get a glimpse of how isolated is this spot, often cut off when it snows, perched bleakly alongside the thin ribbon of road that runs between Postbridge and Moretonhampstead.

The first inn on the site is thought to date from around 1760 and stood on the opposite side of the road to the present 'house' and was known as the 'New House'. That inn would have provided shelter and sustenance for miners and for travellers on the 1772 Moretonhampstead turnpike road, as did the replacement Warren House Inn (once called the Moreton Inn) in later years.

The inn's sign today includes a circular design of three hares, known on Dartmoor as the 'tinners' rabbits'. Rabbits figure large in this area of the moor – a staple of the local diet

and an important source of income for farmers through their meat and fur. Warreners constructed purpose-built 'buries', an early form of factory farming.

Photographs from the late nineteenth century show a moonlike landscape surrounding the inn, scarred by tinners at the Birch Tor and Vitifer mines. Looking east from the inn visitors can still see the remains of gullies and pits – and a little further, at Headland Warren, the outline of four enclosures, each said to be shaped as one of the four suits of

The Warren House Inn surrounded by mine buildings amid the gullies and pits dug by tin miners. This would have been the scene much as Doyle saw it when he walked over to Grimspound from Princetown in 1901.

The Warren House Inn photographed in 1913 and in the state it would have been at the time of Doyle's Dartmoor trip. Thomas Hext, who became landlord in 1882, was still the innkeeper when this photo was taken. His name is on the sign above the door.

33

Right: An early postcard showing tourists arriving at the Warren House Inn by horse drawn carriages c.1920. Above: Sidney Paget's original illustration for The Hound *as it appeared in* The Strand Magazine *in 1901–02. It shows the coachman Perkins pointing out to Dr Watson and his companions their first glimpse of Baskerville Hall.*

The prehistoric enclosure at Grimspound, photographed in 1889, a handful of years before Doyle's visit.

playing cards. The 'Four Aces' as these fields are known, are the cards dropped by Jan Reynolds as the Devil carried him off. Other legends are associated with these fields which actually served as rabbit-proof enclosures associated with warrening. It is almost certain the author of Sherlock Holmes tramped through this area on the way to visit Grimspound in 1901, guided by his friend Bertram Fletcher Robinson.

Reminiscing about his trip around Dartmoor with Doyle, Bertram Fletcher Robinson recalls:

We tramped eastward to the stone fort of Grimspound, which the savages of the Stone Age... raised with enormous labour to act as a haven of refuge from marauding tribes. The twenty feet slabs of granite – how they were ever hauled to their places is a mystery – still encircle the stone huts where the tribe lived. Into one of these Doyle and I walked... It was one of the loneliest spots in Great Britain. Strange legends of lights and figures are told concerning it.

The Warren House c. 1940...

...and today.

Even if Doyle's party did not then stop at the Warren House it certainly would have been visible to them across the valley and today the landlord still guarantees a warm welcome, declaring that the fire in the bar has been burning continuously since 1845!

The Warren House fireplace. A 1940s postcard celebrates the fact the fire has been burning for over 100 years!

POSTBRIDGE

Described as the Heart of Dartmoor for good reason, this little community lies at the centre of the National Park. Philip Weller surmises that the coachman Harry Baskerville is called upon to pick up Doyle and Fletcher Robinson from Grimspound following their fourteen mile trek across the moor. This would mean the horse-drawn coach taking what is now the B3127 from Princetown, travelling via Two Bridges and Postbridge, while returning on that same route.

Photographs from that time show the road as unmetalled which in dry weather would see clouds of dust raised as the open conveyance rattled its way from Grimspound, past the Warren House Inn and down the steep gradient into Postbridge. Here, on the left, the author and his friend would see the 'cyclopean' clapper bridge which, before the turnpike was built, carried the old track over the East Dart. A few yards further and they would pass Greyhound farmhouse which only a few years before had been the Greyhound Inn.

36

"WET" OR "DRY"

"VOTE WET FOR MY SAKE!" "VOTE DRY FOR MINE!"

Shall the Mothers and Children be Sacrificed to the Financial Greed of the Liquor Traffic?

IT IS UP TO YOU, VOTER, TO DECIDE

VOTE . DRY

It is likely that the Greyhound was built in the later half of the eighteenth century. The first recorded innkeeper was Robert Valling who was licenced in 1809, followed by James Davis in 1816, John Lower in 1818 and John Davis again in 1819. By 1839 the inn was run by Joseph Warne before he left to become landlord of the New Inn (Warren House Inn).

The pub that currently serves the thousands of visitors to Postbridge (there's a National Park visitor centre here) is the East Dart. Previously standing here, when Doyle passed through, was Webb's Temperance Hotel opened around 1862 and originally called the New Inn*, presumably to differen-

The Temperance movement became a world wide phenomenon from the 1820s. Here a Women's Christian Temperance Union poster warns Victorians of the perils of drink. Doyle himself was something of an advocate declaring himself for "tolerance, charity, temperance, peace and kindliness."

Webb's Temperance Hotel started life around 1862 as The New Inn, built by local farmer and tin miner, John Webb.

*Not to be confused with the inn of the same name which later became the Warren House. Early records show dozens of New Inns on Dartmoor which appears to be a temporary name applied to any recently licensed hostelry.

The East Dart today, standing on the site of the Temperance Hotel.

tiate it from The Greyhound. Temperance (the shunning of alcohol) was avidly embraced by the Victorian middle classes and as Dartmoor started to become popular as a tourist destination so Webb's was much in demand, as local historian Reg Bellamy records in *The Book of Postbridge*.

> *At this time Postbridge had become very popular and many visitors stayed at 'The Temperance'. They were met at either Moretonhampstead or Princetown railway stations and transported with their luggage in wagonettes belonging either to the hotel or to George French of Greyhound. Others availed themselves of a coach and four which, during the summer months, ran daily from Moretonhampstead to Princetown. It arrived at Postbridge just after 12 noon from Moreton and just after four o'clock from Princetown, announcing its arrival by a postilion blowing his posthorn.*

Postbridge has forever become associated with the legend of The Hairy Hands – a story which post-dates *The Hound of the Baskervilles* by a decade or so and has since become part of Dartmoor's mythology. It is said that around 1910 cyclists approaching Postbridge suddenly felt their handlebars wrenched from their grasp, an event repeated some years later by a motorcyclist who insisted a pair of hairy hands clasped his own and forced him off the road. While we are here celebrating legends, a glimpse at the road surface in some of the early photographs appearing in this book (and the proximity of several inns) might possibly provide a more plausible explanation for suddenly parting company with the road.

TWO BRIDGES

Two Bridges is on the Dart, and is about the middle of this wild uncultivated district; a more dreary situation in winter cannot be imagined... an apology for a farm, around the inn.

T.H. Williams, 1827.

In 1772 when the road from Two Bridges to Moretonhampstead was built, local worthy, Judge Buller of Prince Hall, built two cottages and an inn at what, despite its bleak location, had become an important meeting point of roads crossing the moor north to south, east to west. The inn was the Saracen's Head, a strangely chosen name for a moorland inn – indeed only one other was so named in the whole of Devonshire at that time. However the reason was that the Buller family's crest bore the head of a Saracen.

In times when the moor was less frequented, the inn's proximity to Princetown and the prison must have given

When the Revd John Swete toured Dartmoor in 1797 the turnpike road had been opened and The Saracen's Head built at Two Bridges. In his watercolour the inn stands at the foot of the hill, looking east, where the road sweeps down to the old bridge.

A photograph across to the Saracen's Head taken in snow on Boxing Day 1890. It reveals something of the bleak isolation of this spot as it must have been in the days before motor vehicles.

Also taken in 1890, this photograph of the Saracen's Head shows the view from the direction opposite to that taken in Swete's watercolour. The road to Tavistock winds up the hill beyond the bridge (hidden by the tree), with the track to Princetown branching left halfway up the hill.

passers by and added frisson to their journey, an atmosphere of isolation that infuses the story of *The Hound*. The author Eden Phillpotts whose late Victorian novels are set on Dartmoor was a personal friend and London neighbour of Doyle. Phillpotts' stories abound with local colour and it is quite likely that they had some influence on the author of *The Hound*. Indeed at the time Doyle was staying in Princetown, Phillpotts had put himself up at the Saracen's Head in order to complete his latest work – though there's no evidence of the two men meeting up.

Philpotts fictionalised the inn, referring to it in his novels as the Ring o' Bells, and none too kindly:

Where now stands the best hostelry on Dartmoor, at Two Bridges, nigh Princetown, there existed in the past a little

tavern known as the 'Ring o' Bells'. It scarcely deserved the
name of inn, and was indeed no more than a drinking-house
for the moor-men and a place where horses might be baited
upon their way.

*Two Bridges in the
1930s shortly after
the new bridge was
built.*

Doyle's return from Grimspound would have taken his carriage down the steep hill to the old turnpike bridge that now
stands in the grounds of the Two Bridges
Hotel, a new bridge being constructed
in the 1930s.

*Two Bridges Hotel
today.*

...it was a huge creature, luminous, ghastly, and spectral...

A mile or so from Two Bridges, upstream along the West Dart, walkers come to one of the most atmospheric places on the moor. Here is Wistman's Wood, a dense tangle of twisted ancient dwarf oak trees that appear to grow from the granite boulders that strew the narrow valley. If Arthur Conan Doyle needed a mysterious backdrop to his story of the hellish hound he need look no further.

Wistman's Wood, place of legend.

After painting his tranquil scene at Two Bridges in 1797, the Revd Swete took the narrow path to the wood which he described thus:

> *Silence seemed to have taken up her abode in this sequestered wood – and to a superstitious mind some impression would have occurred approaching to dread, or sacred horror.*

One suggested origin of the wood's name comes from the Devon dialect word Wisht, which refers to being bewitched or haunted, and the legend associated with the wood tells of the Devil hunting human souls with his pack of hellish Wisht Hounds. As Doyle's own description has it:

Opposite: Holmes, Watson and The Hound in Sidney Paget's original illustration for The Hound *as it appeared in* The Strand Magazine *in 1901–02.*

> *...it was a huge creature, luminous, ghastly, and spectral... this dreadful apparition, exactly corresponding to the hell-hound of the legend.*

43

PRINCETOWN

The central square in Princetown photographed in June 1897 precisely four before Doyle's visit. The banner, celebrating Victoria's diamond jubilee, reads 'God Save Our Queen - Long May She Reign. Well played for 60 not out.' The inn, built by Thomas Tyrwhitt in 1795, was originally called The Prince's Arms. On the right is the Duchy Hotel, a much starker facade than its later incarnation but which is how Doyle must have seen it in June 1901.

Dearest of Mams,
Here I am in the highest town in England. Robinson and I are exploring the moor over our Sherlock Holmes book. I think it will work out splendidly – indeed I have already done nearly half of it. Holmes is at his very best, and it is a very dramatic idea – which I owe to Robinson.

We did 14 miles over the moor today and we are now pleasantly weary. It is a great place very sad & wild, dotted with the dwellings of prehistoric man, strange monoliths and huts and graves.

Arthur Conan Doyle writing from Princetown, June 1901

Ironic that the creator of the world's greatest detective should make an error. It's elementary dear reader, Flash in Derbyshire is the highest 'town' in England, a distinction gained by a mere 33 feet it's true; although, by population neither place could claim to be more than a village at the end of the nineteenth century – unless one includes convicts.

Princetown, where Doyle stayed at the Duchy Hotel in June 1901, had by that time only been in existence for a little over 100 years. In 1785 Sir Thomas Tyrwhitt, secretary to the then Prince of Wales, leased a large tract of moorland from the Duchy with the intention of turning the moor into farmland – much as the great 'Improvers' such as Townshend and

Coke had done for Norfolk. His ambition, though thwarted by the unsuitable thin, acid moorland soil, led him to give the name Prince's Town to the handful of buildings he first erected here, including the Plume of Feathers.

But Tyrwhitt's principal claim to fame was his part in the establishment of Dartmoor Prison, siting it on Duchy land and laying the foundation stone in 1806. The prison buildings, grey and austere, live up to the stereotype of a convict gaol – the perfect setting for a Victorian melodrama, although it originally served not as a convict prison but to house French and American prisoners of war captured during the Napoleonic wars. Over 1100 died here from maltreatment and disease before the war prison closed in 1816.

Princetown today. A tourist distination in summer months but isolated. bleak and often cut off in winter.

Princetown seen on 1 June 1898, the same day on which, three years later, Doyle visited. From the Duchy Hotel it is but a short walk to the prison.

The Duchy Hotel

The Plume of Feathers

The Prison

Convicts working under armed guard in the prison quarry c.1900.

A convict on the run, just as Doyle portrays his character, Seldon, in The Hound. *From the* London Illustrated News, *early 1880s*

The prison was not reopened until 1850 when England's jail population was reaching a peak. Transportation of convicts had proved a failure in reducing crime and prison hulks* were overcrowded. So began Dartmoor prison's story as a place of incarceration for criminals, a grim edifice that still draws tourists to gaze at its forbidding walls. Little wonder that Doyle should include the escaped prisoner Seldon in his story of *The Hound*.

The reopening of the prison saw a resurgence in the population of Princetown and the building that had once housed prison guards became a hotel which, along with the Plume of Feathers and, later, the Railway Hotel (the steam line to Princetown opened in 1883), and the Prince of Wales, served the growing numbers of visitors. This former guard house,

The Duchy Hotel at around the time of Doyle's visit in 1901. The facade of the building was much improved in 1908 prior to an official visit by the Prince of Wales.

*Hulks were dismasted men-of-war wooden sailing ships used to as floating prisons in the 18th and 19th centuries. A number were moored in Plymouth.

somewhat austere in appearance, was renamed Rowe's Duchy Hotel after its tenant James Rowe. It was here that, fifty years later, Doyle and Fletcher Robinson took rooms before their exploration of the moor. The hotel by this time was run by Aaron Rowe, grandson of James, and his family. Earlier visitors, as reported in *The Ladies' Companion* of 1860, had expressed severe doubts over the hospitality offered:

> *We called on the landlady, who appeared to combine master and mistress in her bony person, for refreshment, under the denomination of luncheon, which being produced, consisted of some stale bread, bad cheese, and worse beer.*

White's Directory of 1878 lists Henry Coleman Rowe as being landlord of the Railway Hotel. It was built in 1827 and named after the horse tramway which opened in 1823, the steam railway not for another 60 years. Here we see a four-wheeled wagonette similar in design to the vehicle shown in Paget's Strand Magazine *illustrations, and much the same type of conveyance seen in the photograph (opposite) of Harry Baskerville outside his home in the vilage of Ipplepen, this drawn by a single horse.*

The Prince and Princess of Wales attract large crowds outside the Duchy Hotel during their visit to Princetown in 1908.

The Dartmoor National Park Authority High Moorland Visitor Centre has a small display commemorating Sir Arthur Conan Doyle's stay here.

What Doyle thought of his accommodation we'll never know, although his companion, Fletcher Robinson, provides an interesting contrast between the 'bony person' with his own 'cherry-cheeked maid' in recollecting their stay at the Duchy Hotel:

> *The morning after our arrival Doyle and I were sitting in the smoking-room, when a cherry-cheeked maid opened the door and announced 'Visitors to see you, gentlemen.' In marched four men, who solemnly sat down and began to talk about the weather, the fishing in the moor streams and other general subjects.*

These men, it turned out, included the deputy governor, chaplain and the doctor from the prison and had, they said, 'come to meet Mr Sherlock Holmes'.

The Plume of Feathers today, and just beyond the Devil's Elbow (now closed), formerly the Railway Hotel.

While 'Sherlock Holmes' leaves us with no comment on his accommodation, it's clear that Aaron ran a rather more salubrious hotel than his forebears. Indeed his renovation of the hotel in 1908 led to a visit by the Prince and Princess of Wales, with photographs of the event revealing a rather more elegant facade.

In 1941 the hotel became the Dartmoor Prison Officers' Mess and remained so until the early 1990s when it became, and remains, the Dartmoor National Park High Moorland Visitor Centre.

The Prince of Wales, Princetown dates from 1845.

The prison remains although it is no longer home to Britain's most notorious hardened criminals. Princetown itself struggles to find an identity, isolated enough to be intriguing, yet too remote to attract and retain vibrant businesses. A notable exception is The Dartmoor Brewery, established in 1994 and sited near the old railway station. It provides pubs throughout the moor, and further afield, with award winning beers such as Dartmoor Legend and Jail Ale.

Of Princetown inns, only the Plume of Feathers and the Prince of Wales remain. The Railway Hotel was later renamed the Devil's Elbow, so-called after a notorious bend on the old turnpike road, itself now straightened out and gone.

By combining the names of Fox Tor Mire and Grimspound Doyle gave literary life to the great Grimpen Mire. As the evil Jack Stapleton puts it 'A false step yonder means death to man or beast.' Nearby Tor Royal, which the author would have passed on his way to the Mire, is said to be a likely inspiration for Baskerville Hall.

A great deal has been written concerning the 14 mile hike across the moor taken by Doyle and his companion. Doyleian expert Philip Weller proposes the most likely route:

The walk starts at the hotel in Princetown and heads South to Nun's Cross Farm, overlooking Fox Tor Mires. The track then heads Eastwards, along the ridge between Fox Tor Mires and Aune Head Mire, then down the valley of the River Swincombe to Hexworthy. It continues over Laughter Tor, close to the old Laughter Hole Farm, to the hamlet of Bellever. Several tracks are then available for a fairly straight walk to Grimspound.

There's no doubt Doyle was keen to experience some of the wilder parts of the moor and his undoubted awareness of

50

other writers' work, the likes of Phillpotts and Baring-Gould, would have been an inspiration. The latter's *A Book of Dartmoor*, published only a year before Doyle's visit, contained just the sort of material he was looking for:

> *Fox Tor Mire bore a very bad name. The only convict who really got away from Princetown and was not recaptured was last seen taking a bee-line for Fox Tor Mire. The grappling irons at the disposal of the prison authorities were insufficient for the search of the whole marshy tract.*

"That is the Great Grimpen Mire." Paget's illustration in The Hound of the Baskervilles *depicting Dr Watson and Stapleton on the moor.*

Along with 'Grimpen' the author also incorporated actual Dartmoor placenames in his story of *The Hound*, adapting the spelling to suit: Meripit, Bellever, Vixen Tor, Cleft Tor (Cleft Rock), Fernworthy and Lafter Hall (Laughter Hole) among them, several of which places are along the route that he and Fletcher Robinson took from Princetown in June 1901.

From a letter to his mother we have a single first-hand account of the impression the moor left on Doyle that day, a place where solitude can still be found today:

> *In those old days there was evidently a population of very many thousands here, and now you may walk all day and never see one human being. Everywhere there are gutted tin mines.*

"A huge driving wheel and a shaft... Beside it were the crumbling remains of the cottages of miners... in one of these a staple and chain with a quantity of gnawed bones showing where the animal had been confined."

The Hound of the Baskervilles.

The old mine wheel at Whiteworks mine, photographed on 1 June 1889, as Doyle would have seen it – one of his 'gutted mines'. The site overlooks Fox Tor Mire, inspiration for the Grimpen Mire in The Hound of the Baskervilles.

HEXWORTHY

Nun's Cross, the ancient waymarker that gave its name to the farm settlement created here in 1870.

The original Nun's Cross farmhouse built by John Hooper who lived here with his family for almost thirty years. Around 1898, the farm was taken over by Edward Worth who built a new farmhouse alongside the original which then became a cattle shed.

The suggested 14 mile route taken from Princetown by Doyle and Fletcher Robinson in June 1901 would call for stout footwear as the moor could still be treacherously wet in places, even in early summer. Having passed the ruined minewheel at Whiteworks, the two companions, avoiding the impassible ground of Fox Tor Mire at the head of the River Swincombe, would swing south, heading for Nun's Cross Farm. This isolated spot, Weller surmises, fits perfectly the description of the site of wicked Stapleton's home, Merripit House, as detailed in *The Hound*.

While the location seems to fit the bill, the original dwelling at Nun's Cross would hardly do for the sophisticated Stapleton's home although the actual dwelling had been improved from the original makeshift single-storey building known as 'Hooper's Hut', after its tenant farmer John Hooper. The farm stands just a stone's throw from Nun's Cross, also known as Siward's Cross, which has stood here since the thirteenth century and possibly much longer.

Interestingly, in the year in which Doyle took his ramble over the moor, the then tenant of the farm, Edward Worth, applied for permission from the Duchy to build a modern house on the site, the abandoned skeleton of which stands here today. Hooper's old building at first became a cattle shed before it fell into ruin, now evidenced only by traces of its foundations among the reeds.

From this last outpost of habitation Doyle and Robinson would then have taken the moorland track eastwards on the ridge between the mires of Fox Tor and Aune Head. After half a mile or so they would have passed close to the remains of one of the moor's most enigmatic monuments, the cross at Childe's Tomb. Legend has it that this Saxon Lord was lost upon the moor while hunting during a snowstorm. To stay alive he disembowelled his horse and crawled inside the still warm carcase; to no avail for he died at this bleak spot.

Following the ridge, with the Swincombe valley below them, the two men eventually would come in sight of the hamlet of Hexworthy,

Edward Worth's farmhouse, built around 1901, now lies abandoned at the edge of Fox Tor Mire.

Childe's Tomb.

The original Forest Inn c.1890 at which time the tenant landlord was Richard Cleave. In recent correspondence the author learnt from Michael French of Holne that: "The dog, by the way, almost certainly belonged to my great-grandfather who farmed at Hexworthy when the Cleaves were at the Forest Inn." The dog's name was 'Help'.

said by Weller to have put in the author's mind the setting for the village of Grimpen in *The Hound of the Baskervilles.* Even today, the scattering of dwellings certainly fits the narrative:

> *This small clump of buildings here is the hamlet of Grimpen... Within a radius of five miles there are, as you see, only a very few scattered dwellings... Between and around these scattered points extends the desolate, lifeless moor.*

The bridge at Hexworthy c.1890 where the small settlement is a possible candidate for inspiration behind the village of Grimpen in The Hound of the Baskervilles. *An angler stands on the banks of the West Dart.*

Today here stands the forlorn edifice of what was once one of Dartmoor's most popular inns – legendary at least for its remote location in the heart of the moor. Indeed the journey to the inn by car or on foot is what made it a special place to take refreshment.

The Forest Inn, closed at the time this photograph was taken in 2016, was rebuilt in 1916 on the site of the older thatched inn after that burnt down.

The building we see today is somewhat barrack-like, made the more dismal by its current closure as an inn which one can only hope is a temporary circumstance.

The inn started life in the 1850s as an anglers' ale house at which time Richard Cleave applied for a licence to sell ale and liquor. Originally the inn was to be called the 'Forest Arms' but the name was changed a few minutes before applying for the licence, according to historian William Crossing. Along with fisherman, the clientele at this time would have included the tin miners from the nearby Gobbet Plains. As can be seen below, the original building was thatched but a fire in 1913 soon put paid to that. A small section to the right of the old building was left and this was then incorporated into the new refurbished inn which was re-opened in 1916.

The Forest Inn photographed in 1892. It's likely that the figures standing at the door are Richard Cleave and his family whose son, William, took over as landlord in the early 1900s. Richard appears as landlord in Kelly's Directory of 1889, the hamlet called 'Exworthy'.

The Dartmoor Inn, Merrivale, formerly the Merrivale Inn and dating from around 1840, although the settlement here is much earlier.

MERRIVALE

The Dartmoor Inn at Merrivale lies a mile or so north-west of Princetown where the road to Tavistock sweeps down into the valley of the infant River Walkham. On the valley side rises the scar of Merrivale (Duke's) quarry, the workers from which were principal patrons of the Merrivale Inn – now the Dartmoor Inn. It is possible that the placename suggested the name Meripit House to Doyle, as being home of the Stapletons in *The Hound*.

The author would certainly be aware of the area's greatest point of interest, that being the extensive prehistoric remains known as the Merrivale ceremonial complex. Menhirs, stone rows, cairns and other artefacts cover several hectares of open moorland.

One of the stone rows at the prehistoric Merrivale complex. Doyle would be well aware of such features and includes them in his story of The Hound.

56

As the crow flies Merrivale is but a short hop from Wistman's Wood with its tales of hellish hounds. Early travellers on the moor associated these prehistoric stone rows with mysterious druidical rites, as the diarist Eliza Bray, in her book *The Borders of the Tamar and Tavy*, writes:

> *We have on Dartmoor, at a short distance from Merrivale Bridge, and nearly four miles from Wistman's Wood, some very remarkable vestiges of the cursus, or via sacra, used for processions, chariot races, etc., in the Druidical ceremonies.*

In *The Hound of the Baskervilles* the author uses the theatre of this extraordinary landscape as a background in which to set the origins of the hound legend:

> *Now, it opened into a broad space in which stood two of those great stones, still to be seen there, which were set by certain forgotten peoples in the days of old. The moon was shining*

Above: Paget's illustration of the hound among standing stones in the original Baskerville legend.

The Dartmoor Inn pictured around 1900 before the building of a second road bridge.

57

bright upon the clearing, and there in the centre lay the un-happy maid where she had fallen, dead of fear and of fatigue. But it was not the sight of her body, nor yet was it that of the body of Hugo Baskerville lying near her, which raised the hair upon the heads of these three dare-devil roysterers, but it was that, standing over Hugo, and plucking at his throat, there stood a foul thing, a great, black beast, shaped like a hound, yet larger than any hound that ever mortal eye has rested upon.

Two views over Merrivale taken over a hundred years apart. Here we are looking north to-wards the quarry, with the Dartmoor Inn (far right) sit-ting in the valley. The older photo shows the moor as Doyle would have seen it, a once highly industrialised land-scape populated by miners, quarrywork-ers and their fami-lies. Much has changed; the quarry closed and the line of workers' cottages demolished. The road that once passed in front of the inn now crosses a wider bridge and the older buildings, standing on the inn's left, have been replaced. On the road from Princetown to Merrivale, at Rundlestone, there once stood the Rundlestone Inn where the landlord in 1850 was William Friend.

THE NORTHERN MOOR

OKEHAMPTON

Much conjecture has been expended on the origins of *The Hound of the Baskervilles* – even much hot air spent on who actually wrote the story. Doyle himself insisted on giving credit to his friend Fletcher Robinson for inspiration behind the tale, as he makes clear in a letter to the editor of *The Strand Magazine* in which the story first appears:

> *I have the idea for a real creeper for "The Strand"... There is one stipulation. I must do it with my friend Fletcher Robinson, and his name must appear with mine. I can answer for the yarn being all my own in my own style without dilution, since your readers like that. But he gave me the central idea and the local colour, and so I feel his name must appear.*

Notwithstanding the help from his friend, it's clear that the author was something of a magpie when it came to constructing his stories, picking up treasures here and there to add verisimilitude to his writings. Much as he created real-sounding places by combining elements of actual place-names, so he also picked up local legends from throughout the country to help construct his 'beast'. Time in Norfolk had acquainted him with Black Shuck – the phantom dog haunt-

The gaunt ruins of Okehampton Castle from where the ghost of Lady Howard and her fire-breathing black hound emerged each evening.

ing the wilds of that county – while similar legends exist throughout the country. Devon and Dartmoor, it seems, have more than their fair share, 'at least fifty' the noted folklorist and historian Theo Brown records in her book *Devon Ghosts*.

Prominent among these is the legend of Lady Howard of Fitzford near Tavistock, a tale recorded by the Revd Sabine Baring-Gould in his *Songs of the West* published in 1891:

Okehampton Castle today.

The Revd Swete's view of Okehampton Castle in 1797.

> *Lady Howard was a person of strong will and imperious temper. She bore the reputation of having been hard-hearted in her lifetime. For some crime she had committed (nobody knew what), she was said to be doomed to run in the shape of a hound from the gateway of Fitzford to Okehampton Park, between the hours of midnight and cock-crowing, and to return with a single blade of grass in her mouth to the place whence she had started; and this she was to do till every blade was picked, when the world would be at an end.*

Looking north along Fore Street in Okehampton c.1890.

A number of variations of the story exist, one relating that Lady Howard travelled from Okehampton Castle to Launceston every night in a coach made of her husband's bones, driven by a headless coachman, the carriage preceded by a fire-breathing black hound, the sight of which heralded a death in the family of anyone witnessing the event. A tale which is closely echoed in Doyle's description of his own beast:

> *A hound it was, an enormous coal-black hound, but not such a hound as mortal eyes have ever seen. Fire burst from its open mouth, its eyes glowed with a smouldering glare, its muzzle and hackles and dewlap were outlined in flickering flame. Never in the delirious dream of a disordered brain could anything more savage, more appalling, more hellish be conceived than that dark form and savage face which broke upon us out of the wall of fog.*

While Okehampton lies a little outside the boundary of the National Park, it is very much a moorland town and it has

Fore Street in Okehampton today. The White Hart Hotel on the right, according to folklorist Theo Brown, has a ghost called Peter, said to be the spirit of a boy forever searching for his murdered mother.

Okehampton railway station on the L&SWR line that skirted northern Dartmoor at the time The Hound of the Baskervilles *was published. Opened in 1871 the line now operates heritage railway services.*

Capturing Dartmoor at its atmospheric best this 1890 photograph by Robert Burnard 'taken on a stormy evening' shows a steam train crossing Meldon viaduct under a brooding sky. This is the North Devon line taken by Jack Stapleton in The Hound.

one further connection to *The Hound of the Baskervilles*. At the end of the story, where Sherlock Holmes is reflecting on events with Watson he discusses the fiendish Jack Stapleton's return to Dartmoor having purchased his giant hound in London:

> *He brought it down by the North Devon line and walked a great distance over the moor so as to get it home without exciting any remarks.*

This railway line, eventually part of the London & South Western Railway, ran from Exeter, via Crediton, then on to Okehampton, Meldon and Lydford. Thereafter it joined the South Devon Railway to reach Plymouth, via Tavistock.

Railways play a significant role in the development of *The Hound* story, while the inns and post houses that served the railways, were part of the late Victorian world that the readers of *The Strand Magazine* inhabited. The author's careful setting of his detective stories against the background of the technological developments of the age helped bring them to life in the minds of his avid readership.

And Okehampton had no shortage of inns, as one local author records:

The London Inn, Okehampton today.

> *Besides the White Hart the town was well supplied with taverns, inns and public houses. There was the Butcher & Ox in Fore Street run by John Palmer, the Golden Lion kept by Richard Heanes, and John Ponsford's hotel of course, the Red Lion, run by Richard Rich, Joseph Drew's Plume of Feathers, the Town Arms owned by Richard Lillicrap, Will Soper's Barnstaple Inn down North Lane, the Kings Arms, run by Geake Digory in Back Street and John Palmer's New Inn. By East Bridge, one arrived at the Fountain occupied by John Stanley in East Town, the Exeter Inn, held by William Morcombe, and the Star belonging to Joseph Seymour.*

The Plume of Feathers c.1900, when Thomas Kennard was landlord.

*The Fountain Inn
Okehampton in the
1920s and today.*

Thus had the wicked Stapleton wished for a pint or two in Okehampton before he set off across the moor with his hound, he would have ample choice of hostelry.

BELSTONE

In 1893 *Chambers' Journal* published anonymously a short story called 'A Tale of Dartmoor Fog'. While it is almost certain that Sir Arthur Conan Doyle was not its author, he had written for that magazine both before and after that date and is likely to have read it. It has even been suggested by Philip Weller that its author was in fact none other than Doyle's friend Bertram Fletcher Robinson whose knowledge of the moor is reflected in the detailed description of actual places included in the tale.

*Belstone c.1920. The
building on the left
became The Tors
Hotel.*

The Tors Hotel today.

The story involves the escape of a prisoner from Dartmoor who, having been chased by a spectral apparition ends up disappearing in a moorland pool. The story has obvious resonances with *The Hound*, not least through the escaped prisoner and his mirey end. The tale ends as a group of moormen and soldiers meet up at Belstone 'clustered about the one public house'.

The inn at Belstone today is The Tors which Weller says replaced the original inn, gutted by fire in 1896. *White's Directory* of 1850 however gives George Reddaway as licensee of the New Inn at 'Belston' – 'a small village picturesquely set... where the druids had a temple for the worship of the sun.' In 1878 the New Inn landlord is William Brock, and in 1889 William Reddaway.

Sun worshipping probably refers to the Nine Stones circle on the side of Belstone Tor, otherwise known as the Nine Maidens which, according to legend, are the petrified remains of nine girls turned to stone for daring to dance on a Sunday.

The former telegraph office in what was the Zion Chapel in Belstone still retains its enamel sign over the door. It closed in 2002. Doyle makes much of the use of this 'modern' form of communication to move the story of The Hound along.

A place of legend; the Nine Maidens actually number around sixteen stones. It is a kerb cairn, a likely burial site dating to the Bronze Age.

65

Sticklepath c.1900.

STICKLEPATH

Travelling with his hound, Waterloo Station would have provided Stapleton a direct line back to Dartmoor via Salisbury and Exeter.

Official carrier for the London & Southwestern Railway, James Knapman travelled from Okehampton to Dartmoor's outlying villages carrying goods delivered by rail.

Sticklepath sits just east of Belstone on the old coaching road that carriers and stagecoaches plied in the days of horse-drawn vehicles. The route skirts the northern edge of the moor and the villages that lie along it retain something of the atmosphere and character of those early days, more so now that the A30 dual carriageway bypasses them.

Holidaymakers in the 1950s and 60s taking the old A30 route into Cornwall will have mixed memories of lines of cars slowly winding their way through Sticklepath and grinding up the steep hill beyond – stricken cars at the side of the road, bonnets-up, steam rising.

The North Devon railway that we suppose Jack Stapleton took with his hound passed north of Sticklepath, its closest station at Belstone Corner (Sampford Courtney), a four mile hike but certainly the most unobtrusive way for a man and a terrifying hound to avoid public attention.

In the days before cars the road through the village served as the main route north of Dartmoor. For stage coaches and particularly for carriers' carts this was a well-frequented if arduous thoroughfare serving the outlying farms and hamlets. Such was the state of the roads and their steepness that travel was slow, with a consequent need for frequent stopping places, to take refreshment and to change horses.

At the turn of the nineteenth century Sticklepath provided two excellent establishments for travellers, the Devonshire Inn, landlord Richard Knapman, and the Taw River Inn run by William James Drew. *White's Directory* of 1850 lists also the Cornish Arms.

The Devonshire Inn c.1900.

The Taw Valley Inn (on left) 1910.

67

Looking west past the Taw River Inn c.1925.

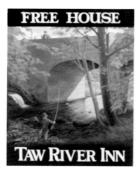

The same view today.

The village is associated with the legend of The Honest Man, the name given to a standing stone bearing strange incised markings which some authorities have attributed to the Bronze Age, some to Druids, and one to 'a rural stone-masons's doodling'.

It is said that the stone is named after the deeds of a Good Samaritan who fought off thieves who had robbed a man near the spot where the stone stands.

The Honest Man.

The inscribed stone sited near the Lady Well photographed c.1910.

The view east in Sticklepath c. 1910 with the Devonshire inn on the right.

The same view today..

It's possible of course the name is simply ironic, relating to the saying 'Let me show you an honest man...' (a dumb stone that cannot lie), an interpretation which suits the laconic humour of locals.

A similarly carved stone stands nearby at Lady Well, an ancient watering place from which villagers drew their supplies and which in later times was enclosed in a roughly hewn grotto with a lintel bearing the inscription

Sticklepath in 1900, around the time The Hound of the Baskervilles *was first published.*

'Lady Well, drink & be thankful.' This has something of the hallmarks of an attempt to draw tourists to the spot, but ancient wells throughout the country were once revered and old photographs show this location as having an air of remote mystery.

Claims have also been made to link Sticklepath to another of Dartmoor's enduring legends, that of Uncle Tom Cobley, Jan Pearse and Co., and their grey mare. A story more closely associated with Widecombe-in-the-Moor, the link with Sticklepath is derived from a gravestone here, erected in memory of one Tom Pearse who died in 1875. There is no definitive evidence to connect this character to the famous song which formed part of the *Songs and Ballads of the West* book of folksongs collected by Revd Sabine Baring Gould published between 1889–91.

An elegant Edwardian Lady visits the Lady Well.

A second inscribed stone stands close to the Lady Well in this superb photograph dating from around 1900.

Tom Pearce, Tom Pearce, lend me your grey mare.
All along, down along, out along lea.
For I want for to go to Widecombe Fair,
With Bill Brewer, Jan Stewer, Peter Gurney,
Peter Davy, Dan'l Whiddon, Harry Hawke,
Old Uncle Tom Cobley and all,
Old Uncle Tom Cobley and all.

SOUTH ZEAL & SOUTH TAWTON

These two moorland hamlets lie cheek-by-jowl inside the northern boundary of the Dartmoor National Park. Farming and mining sustained these villages, the latter occupation seeing the populations rise dramatically during the nineteenth century with all the associated trades that come with such expansion.

As historian Ursula Radford has put it:

> *Where competition did run riot around 150 years ago was in the catering trade, or 'victualing' provision. South Tawton and South Zeal boasted at least eight public houses c.1850–1870.*

In 1850 these included the Kings Arms, the Lamb Inn, the Seven Stars, the Victoria, the London Inn and the Oxenham Arms. Forty years after this date the White Horse and the Rising Sun additionally helped keep the thirsty miners in ale.

Doyle refers to the 'gutted mines' on Dartmoor seen during his visit, and while many were still in production into the twentieth century, the heyday of mining was indeed over and the 'boom towns' such as South Zeal were returning to their former sleepier days.

Of the many former hostelries three survive, one of which, the Oxenham Arms, is the source of an enduring legend; and

Customers and staff outside the Seven Stars Inn, South Tawton c.1920.

The Oxenham Arms early 1900s.

as with legends of *The Hound*, involves the appearance of a phantom animal presaging untimely death. Such tales, as with Norfolk's Black Shuck, together inspired Doyle's portrayal of his hound. William Dutt, writing in the year *The Hound of the Baskervilles* was published, described Black Shuck's appearance:

South Zeal in the 1890s. The sign for the London Inn, which closed in 1906, can be seen on the thatched building on the left

> *He takes the form of a huge black dog, and prowls along dark lanes and lonesome field footpaths, where, although his howling makes the hearer's blood run cold, his footfalls make no sound... it is even said that to meet him is to be warned that your death will occur before the end of the year.*

The Oxenham Arms today. Built into the fabric of the building there is said to be a prehistoric menhir. It's certainly a feature worth the visitor seeking out.

With the Oxenham Arms it is a bird that was said to appear before the death of the young James Oxenham who, in 1635, fell sick and died but not before 'two whom two days before hee yeelded up his soul to God, there appeared the likeness of a bird with a white breast, hovering over him.' In later years other members of the family, whose coat of arms the inn still bears, were also visited by the phantom bird shortly before dying.

South Zeal today. Compare this with the view on the previous page and a number of the original buildings are still easily identifiable, including the old London Inn, now a private dwelling.

One of the survivors of at least eight pubs formerly in South Tawton and South Zeal, the Kings Arms is said to have been the favourite haunt of farmers and miners.

Thankfully the Kings Arms at the top of South Zeal village has also survived the closures, not least as the building itself offers so much of what one imagines a typical country inn should be. Probably dating from the 16th century, the position of the inn at the head of the steep hill descending into the village meant it left the coaching trade to the Oxenham Arms and the London Inn. George Knapman was host here for most of the latter half of the nineteenth century.

WHIDDON DOWN

This was alway an important meeting place where the ancient route skirting the northern moor met the north-south road along the moor's eastern edge. Even today there is not much settlement here but its strategic position made it an ideal location for an inn. The construction of the A30 dual carriageway has moved the principal junction farther north but the road remains busy, bringing passing trade to what is now called the Post Inn.

The village takes its name from the Whiddon (Whyddon) family who owned a substantial house and much land hereabouts from at least the fifteenth century; wealthy enough certainly to create their own deer park.

The legend associated with the family revolves around one Mary Whiddon who rejected a fervent suitor in favour of another. In Chagford parish church, on the day of her wedding in October 1641, Mary was brutally stabbed in a jealous rage by her former lover, and died on the altar steps. A memorial stone in the church includes the lines:

But dry thine eyes why wilt thou weep
Such damselles doe not die, but sleep.

Looking west from the crossroads at Whiddon Down in the 1930s. This is the road that once took all traffic west from Exeter towards Okehampton along the northern edge of the moor. The Post Office Inn, on the left, offers 'Good accommodation for tourists'.

The Post Office Inn in the 1950s and, with a slight name change, the Post Inn today.

The story is said to have been the inspiration behind R.D. Blackmore's *Lorna Doone*.

In 1850 Thomas Hooper was landlord of the Post Office Inn, while John Powlesland is recorded as running a 'beer-house' here. In 1889 the landlord of The Post Office Inn was Francis Woolland.

DREWSTEIGNTON

As with fairy tales and folklore, many of our legends have elemental truths contained within them, and which in their retelling provided salutory lessons, especially when told to children, to warn of real dangers. Ferocious hounds are found in myths dating from Greek and Roman times; best known Cerberus, the 'Hound of Hades' who guarded the gates of hell. In European myths hounds were often part of a hellish hunt, fiendish animals reeking of brimstone and led by the devil in human guise.

Doyle recognised the primal horror that his hound would raise among his readers, a fear that drew upon centuries of humans living under threat of attack from wild beasts.

Hercules capturing the three-headed hound from hell, Cerberus, depicted on an ancient Greek vase.

Drewsteignton is included here for it is in the dense woodland that blankets the valley of the River Teign that the last wolf in Devon is said to have been killed. If so, this post-dates the received wisdom of the wolf's disappearance in England by several hundred years. In his book *High Dartmoor*, Eric Hemery recounts:

> *The Rev. Welldon Peek wrote that, as a boy in 1894, he was told by George Counter, then aged sixty, that his grandfather (in his nineties when Counter was a boy) used to tell him about wolves in the woods around Drewsteignton when he was a young man and how people were 'afeard of 'un'.*

Deep woodland clads the steep valley sides of the Teign Gorge above Sharp Tor

Whatever the truth of this, the fact that children were still being brought up on stories of wolves lurking in woods not far from their homes, gives insight into the public reaction to *The Hound of the Baskervilles* at the time of publication. In 1901 Dartmoor was still considered a dangerous wilderness by outsiders – the perfect setting for Doyle's infernal beast.

Eric Hemery also refers to the tradition that the last wolf on Dartmoor was killed in Brimpts Wood in 1780.

Of the four established inns in Drewsteignton, three now survive, being the Drewe Arms in the village square, the Fingle Bridge Inn and the Sandy Park. In identifying the history of the naming of these inns there's a mystery worthy of Sherlock Holmes The Old Inn, now a restaurant bearing the name, is recorded from the late 1800s when the landlord was William Ellis. The New Inn, appears earlier; we know in 1850 the landlord was William Smith. This later became the Druid Arms and eventually the Drewe Arms. The Fingle Bridge Inn, sitting at the edge of the River Teign, was originally a tea shop, and for many years called the Anglers' Rest.

As was common around the moor up to the mid 1800s, there were several places named as 'beerhouses' in the records which, along with Church Houses, brewed and sold beer. In Devon, cider was the drink of choice and farmers tended orchards and kept presses from which they made significant quantities of rough cider. Poorer, weaker cider, often known as small cider, was the drink of the common man and was even paid to farm labourers as part of their wages. They were given up to six pints a day, and this could increase to twenty pints or more at harvest time.

Primal fear of wolves lingered for years after the beasts became extinct in Britain.

The square Drewsteignton c.1900. The Old Inn is the white building centre distance. What is now the Drewe Arms (right) has its signboard painted out, probably when it was being renamed the Druid Arms.

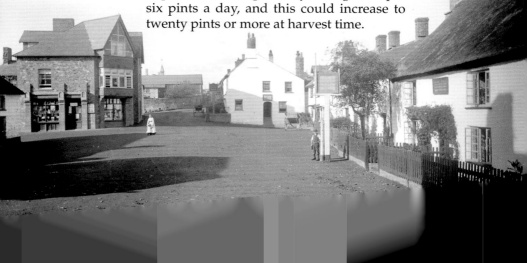

Around 1906 the New Inn changed its name to the Druid Arms, possibly a reference to nearby Spinsters Rock, a neolithic chambered tomb, and the type of antiquity that early writers associated with the druids. The name was short-lived for in 1910, the wealthy Julius Drewe bought land in the area on which to build Castle Drogo – an edifice which literally cemented his family name to what he considered his ancestral home. The Druid Arms now became the Drewe Arms, with a massive wrought iron sign bearing the arms of the Drewe family a surviving legacy.

A similar view to the one opposite but taken a few years later. Here the landlord Alfred Mudge, who became licensee in 1906, stands in front of the former New Inn, renamed the Druid Arms.

Originally known as the Anglers' Rest, the Fingle Bridge Inn grew out of a Victorian tea room which previously occupied the same site.

79

The porch where the poet Sydney Godolphin died. The Three Crowns seen from the churchyard.

CHAGFORD

Shortly before Doyle's visit to Dartmoor, the splendidly named Dartmoor Exploration Committee, whose members included Revd Sabine Baring-Gould and photographer Robert Burnard, began excavations at Fernworthy. Doyle attaches this placename to 'a small hamlet' in *The Hound of the Baskervilles,* home of Mr Frankland of Lafter Hall. Fernworthy reservoir now covers the site.

Fernworthy lies in Chagford Parish, some distance from the main action in *The Hound,* but a plausible location from its description in the book. Its connection to contemporary archaeological discoveries in the 1890s also chimes with the reactions of Holmes and Watson in their own 'discovery' of the ancient of hut circles on the moor.

The window of the Chagford Inn, formerly The Bakers Arms and then the Bullers Arms.

Chagford is one of the principal settlements on the moor and, as such, has been amply provided for in regard to inns and taverns. One of the oldest, the Royal Oak, had fallen by the wayside by the end of the 1800s but the Bakers Arms (later the Bullers Arms), the Globe, the Kings Arms, the Ring of Bells and the Three Crowns were all then in business.

The legend of Mary Whiddon and her murder in Chagford's St Michael's church is covered earlier and it is to an inn that the town's other historic story of note is attached. This relates to the Three Crowns and dates back to 1643

Looking west along High Street around 1930 and the same view today. The Globe Inn is on the left and the granite porch of the Three Crowns beyond. Out of view but on the same side of the street is the Ring of Bells and further along, in Mill Street, is the Chagford Inn.

during the English Civil War. It was here that the 33 year old Royalist, Sydney Godolphin, was shot during a brief skirmish with Parliamentary troops, dying in the granite porch of the inn, which his ghost is said to haunt.

The railway never came to Chagford, and although the line was proposed in 1883 it was never built, and thus the place retained its air of splendid moorland isolation long after its counterparts on the western moor became urbanised.

Sandy Park today and as it looked around 1890 when Richard Brock was landlord.

Midway between Chagford and Drewsteignton (and actually in this parish), lying at the crossroad on the A382, sits the Sandy Park Inn and included here as it has much to recommend it, not least from its picturesque exterior and cottage-like homely bars.

THROWLEIGH

It might be an exaggeration to call Wonson a hamlet; a tiny oasis between the villages of Gidleigh and Throwleigh. The Northmore Arms is one of the places that seem always difficult to find however many times one visits – but always worthwhile finding. The inn bears the arms of the Northmore family who owned the manor hereabouts. In the early 1700s, William Northmore MP, a notorious gambler, staked an enormous fortune on the ace of diamonds, and lost. He had an image of the card painted on his bedroom wall and is said to have cursed it each night instead of praying.

The Northmore Arms was earlier called the New Inn and in 1850 was run by Gustavus Gidley. It took over as the local' from The Royal Oak in Throwleigh where George Gidley had been landlord. At the time The Hound was written John Dicker ran the inn.

THE WESTERN MOOR

TAVISTOCK

*It had evidently set in wet, so, with heads bowed to the blast
and collars buttoned about our necks we staggered along in
the direction in which we knew that Tavistock lay. I don't
think any of us are ever likely to forget that eight-mile trudge.*

Sir Arthur Conan Doyle, 1882.

In 1882, aged twenty-three, Doyle joined the medical practice of George Turnavine Budd in Plymouth. It was also the year in which the budding author's article *Dry Plates on a Wet Moor* was published in the prestigious *British Journal of Photography*. The piece is a humorous description of an abortive photo excursion to Dartmoor and contains some interesting passages that throw light on to Doyle's later attachment to the moor – and his fondness for public houses.

The photographic adventurers comprised the author and two companions, the 'Commodore' and the 'Genius' whose journey begins in the salubrious Royal Hotel in Plymouth:

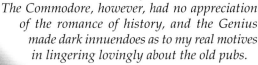

*I should like to have spent the whole day in the old historical
sea town... It was strange to see the very alehouses still standing upon the Barbican, in which the bearded and bejewelled
filibusters of Drake and Hawkins had squandered doubloons...
The Commodore, however, had no appreciation
of the romance of history, and the Genius
made dark innuendoes as to my real motives
in lingering lovingly about the old pubs.*

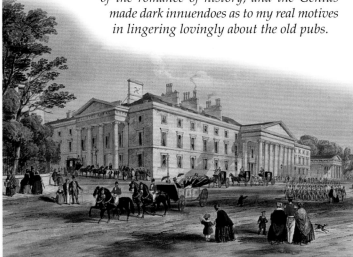

*Foulston's Royal
Hotel, Theatre and
Assembly Rooms,
Plymouth c.1820.*

83

"Rugged tors and tangled vegetation," Sheepstor from the west.

The journey on foot takes them out of the city following what is now the route of the A386. Doyle's article continues with a description of the moor that has resounding echoes in *The Hound of the Baskervilles* published almost twenty years later:

Signposts fixed where every sheep path departs from the main track.

> *As we advanced the character of the scenery began to change. Rugged "tors" and tangled masses of half-withered vegetation shut us in, and the narrow road wound through a wilderness in which the only living creatures seem to be a few half-starved Devonshire sheep, who eyed us curiously, as if speculating upon our motives for intruding upon their domains. Wild and stern as was the scene there was a certain rough beauty in it all... The enormous number of white sign posts fixed at the angle where every sheep-path departed from the main track told a grim story of the byegone dangers of the Moor — where men had wandered in circles until they had*

dropped dead of hunger and fatigue. Indeed, with all these precautions, during the last twelve months there have been at least three cases of individuals having met with a similar fate.

The perfect setting indeed for the most famous detective story in history.

Built on the wealth of mining, nineteenth century Tavistock had been at the centre of the richest copper mines in the world. The Dukes of Bedford who controlled much of this bounty had done much to create the town that Doyle and his companions walked into on that wet August evening:

> *When we found ourselves at last in the streets of the pictur-esque town... three sorrier figures could not have been picked out in the length and breadth of England.*

Having stayed at Plymouth's premier hotel perhaps the trio took pity on themselves by taking the best rooms in Tavis-tock, at the Bedford Hotel. Not that there was any shortage of places to stay, for the wealth of this market town saw a proliferation of inns during the eighteenth and nineteenth centuries. Town centre hostelries included the Tavistock Inn in Brook Street, the Union Inn in King Street, Ordulph Arms in Pym Street, and the Cornish Arms and the Queens Head in West Street.

The Commercial Inn Bedford Square c.1900.

Having his first taste of Dartmoor weather the author returns to Plymouth with his companions:

> *With heavy hearts we were forced to acknowledge that the game was up, and a hermetically-sealed four-wheeler bore us off with our effects to catch the midday train for home.*

SOURTON

The New Inn as it looked in the early 1900s. It had earlier been the Golden Fleece and is now The Highwayman.

The western border of the National Park north of Tavistock extends to Okehampton and roughly follows the old coaching road (now the A386) along which lie several inns.

Most northerly is the village of Sourton where the road meets the ancient east–west route skirting the moor. *White's Directory* of 1850 lists Mary Dark as victualler of the Seven Stars, William Dark as a 'beer seller' and Richard Horn as landlord of the New Inn (formerly the Golden Fleece). Horn combined his occupation with farming as did Joseph Ball who was running

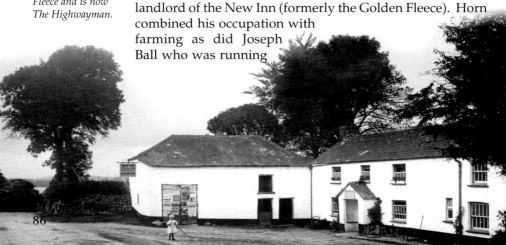

the New Inn around the time Doyle was writing of his trip to Tavistock.

Despite its long history it is in relatively recent times that the inn, in 1959 renamed The Highwayman, acquired legendary status through the efforts of Rita and Buster Jones who began transforming the building into a fantasy olde worlde inn, adding an accretion of elements that make it a truly exceptional place to visit.

The Highwayman Inn today. A curiousity that draws many tourists to its remarkable doors.

LYDFORD

A guidebook of 1850 describes Dartmoor as being 200 000 acres 'of which the most dreary part is in Lydford parish'. Ideal territory for legends and, indeed, an early BBC made-for-TV adaptation of *The Hound of the Baskervilles* was partly shot in Lydford, with scenes outside the Castle Inn.

Built as a prison, Lydford Castle was notorious for its dungeons and for the rule of law that proposes criminals should first hang and then be tried!

87

Lydford from an engraving by Samuel Prout, 1810.

In 1238 the Forest of Dartmoor, including Lydford castle was granted by Henry III to his brother, Richard Earl of Cornwall, and they remain with the Duchy today.

In the sixteenth century the area was inhabited by a notorious band of outlaws known by the name of Gubbins:

> *They are a peculiar of their own making, exempt from Bishop, Archdeacon, and all authority either ecclesiastical or civil. They live in cotts (rather holes than houses) like swine, having all in common, multiplied, without marriage, into many hundreds. Their language is the drosse of the dregs of the vulgar Devonian...*

An early postcard of Lydford with the Castle Inn just visible at the end of the street.

Looking down into the chasm through which the River Lyd cascades.

The later stone bridge spanning the gorge.

This band of near-naked savages ravaged the region until, by the mid 1600s, they appear to have been extinguished. They appear throughout the literature of Dartmoor and it is quite probable that Doyle drew upon these stories as when Dr Watson describes Seldon, the escaped prisoner:

> *Foul with mire, with a bristling beard, and hung with matted hair, it might well have belonged to one of those old savages who dwelt in the burrows on the hillsides.*

The Lydford Gorge is today in the hands of the National Trust and visitors can walk alongside the broiling waters of the Lyd to visit The White Lady Waterfall and to stand beneath the yawning jaws of the 'Lydford Leap', both features inspiring local legends.

Four inns lie within a short compass of the village of Lydford itself. From the top: the Castle Inn, the Dartmoor Inn, the Bearslake Inn, the Fox and Hounds.

The latter involves a lone traveller on horseback who arrives at the inn having crossed the moor in darkness with a storm raging. With incredulity the locals ask how he crossed the gorge, for they know the bridge has been washed away, and the stranger recalls how his horse suddenly leapt through the darkness – clearing the chasm and saving the traveller's life.

The Castle Inn, as its name suggests, nestles in the lee of those ancient walls. It dates from the sixteenth century and is one of four hostelries that lie within easy reach of the gorge.

MARY TAVY

An engraving of the earlier wooden bridge said to have been lost in a storm.

The world's largest copper mine, Wheal Friendship, once made this a thriving community more akin to a scene from the Wild West as miners flooded in to take advantage of this bonanza. In the 1850 the population of Tavy St Mary (including Blackdown which lies alongside), as it was then known, stood at 1500 – the majority working the mines.

While it is almost certain that many cider and beer houses sprang up during these boom years, two licensed inns are listed in the directories of 1850, the Buller Arms and the Royal Standard. In 1898 the Royal Standard and the Mary Tavy Inn are listed, the latter being the original Buller Arms.

Miners were sometimes paid with 'tokens', coin minted by mine owners, which could be traded for goods in local shops and inns (invariably in the hands of the mine owners). Locally these were called Tavistock tokens. Some were minted for exclusive use in inns, known as tavern tokens.

A miners' penny

The Royal Standard.

91

The Buller Arms seen in 1903. The same building today but now called the Mary Tavy Inn.

Legend has it that a notorious Highwayman by the name of Captain Jack once prowled the lanes here. Captured, he was sentenced to hang in a gibbet on nearby Gibbet Hill, his body displayed to deter others from crime.

Originally called the New Inn, and named as such in *White's Directory* of 1850, the isolated little inn at nearby Horndon is now called The Elephant's Nest.

PETER TAVY

As with its neighbour, Peter Tavy found itself the focus of immigration as miners, and others with an enterprising eye, flocked to work in the local mines. The lane leading to the Peter Tavy Inn still retains enough of the atmosphere of those times for the visitor to conjure up the frantic hubbub of workers on their way to the mines; the unremitting grind

The Peter Tavy Inn in the 1930s and (below) the Inn today.

of work underground, their exhausted emergence into the raw beauty of the moorland landscape.

In 1850 the 'victualler' at the Peter Tavy Inn is one Thomas Ware, a family name recorded in Devon in pre-Conquest times. By the late 1800s Robert Prout ran the inn, combining his landlord duties with his trade as a blacksmith.

A faint echo of convict Seldon's escape recounted in *The Hound of the Baskervilles* is paralleled in the 1960s when notorious henchman of the Kray twins, Frank 'Mad Axeman' Mitchell is said to have frequented the inn. Acutely mentally unstable, Frank was treated with some leniency during his life sentence in H.M. Prison Dartmoor, breeding budgies and being allowed remarkable freedom when on working parties around the moor. This included visits to the Peter Tavy Inn, his bar bill picked up by the twins who later helped 'spring' him from prison before murdering him.

How the Illustrated London News *depicted a Dartmoor convict's escape in the 1880s.*

The Whitchurch Inn today.

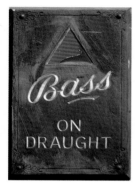

Britain's oldest trademark, Bass Brewery's red triangle was first registered in 1875. Here is an early slate plaque on the wall of the Whitchurch Inn.

The Whitchurch inn c.1880 when William Mashford was landlord.

WHITCHURCH

As we have seen with the excursion in *Dry Plates on a Wet Moor*, Arthur Conan Doyle's acquaintance with Dartmoor provided the substance for stories written almost twenty years in advance of *The Hound*. Among his influences would have been writers such as Revd Sabine Baring-Gould, Eden Phillpotts and Frederick Adye. Adye's novel *Queen of the Moor*, published in 1885, bears a number of similarities to *The Hound* both in its setting and in parts of the narrative, but in particular to Doyle's short story 'Silver Blaze' published in *The Strand Magazine* in 1892.

In *Queen of the Moor* Adye refers to the training of race-horses on Whitchurch Down while 'Silver Blaze' involves Sherlock Holmes and Watson investigating activities at racing stables on the edge of the moor, the location, disguised as 'King's Pyland', but fitting the description of Whitchurch:

The country round is very lonely, but about half a mile to the north there is a small cluster of villas which have been built

by a Tavistock contractor for the use of invalids and others who may wish to enjoy the pure Dartmoor air. Tavistock itself lies two miles to the west, while... in every other direction the moor is a complete wilderness, inhabited only by a few roaming gypsies.

Whitchurch viewed from the south, early 1900s. Note the railway line which ran from Tavistock to Plymouth and which Doyle would have taken on his return from Tavistock in 1882.

Indeed as early as 1753 the Duke of Bedford had donated 'a silver pint mug and a silver tumbler to be run for by horses and some other prizes to be sported for on Whitchurch Down'.

For those providing hospitality, such as the Whitchurch Inn and Grenofen's Halfway House (now a café), these races must have provided wonderful business. Of these inns the former is by far the most venerable, a medieval hostelry owned by the church and most likely brewing its own ale.

YELVERTON

Doyle's walking tour from Plymouth to Tavistock in 1882, along with companions, the Commodore and the Genius, would have taken him through Yelverton. Black's *Guide to Devonshire* of around this date describes it thus:

Yelverton stands on Roborough Down, an open common where villas are springing up, as the place comes into favour as a resort for Plymouth people. The road to Plymouth is 6 miles but the railway nearly twice as long, winding up in the manner of a miniature St Gothard line.

95

The Rock Inn Yelver-
ton c.1890.

The inns at this time are listed as the Rock Inn, the Leg of Mutton and the intriguingly named Barron's American Hotel and Boarding House, but it is the railway that links us to the story of *The Hound*.

Fond as he was of railways, which figure greatly in many of his stories, in his visit to Princetown to collect material for writing his most famous work, the author chooses not to arrive by train. However the line does feature briefly in the 1931 film version of *The Hound* which has a shot of the distant train rounding Kings Tor. The train then pulls in at 'Baskerville Halt', actually Lustleigh Station, situated on the other side of the moor!

Princetown railway
station c.1910

The 1939 film of *The Hound of the Baskervilles* depicts the episode in which Holmes and Watson leave Baskerville Hall,

Sherlock Holmes and Dr Watson on the Okehampton train from the 1931 film of The Hound of the Baskervilles. *But is the view from the window really Dartmoor?*

and take the train to Okehampton in order to fool the murderer into believing they are leaving for London. The two men sit in a studio mock up of a railway carriage while back projection of what looks remarkably like the high moorland landscape rolls by outside the window.

The line from Yelverton to Princetown meandered on a single track for a little over ten miles with halts at Dousland, Ingra Tor and Sheepstor. This line branched from the South Devon & Tavistock Railway which ran north out of Yelverton through an impressive 641 yard tunnel.

MEAVY

This small settlement lies a mile or so east of Yelverton and the inn here is named after the village's most famous feature, the Meavy Oak. Legend has it that the oak was planted in the time of King John and was the centre of various rites and festivals held here. As with other great trees, notably the Cross Tree (or Dancing Tree) in Moretonhampstead, a platform was set up in the tree's branches on which feasting and dancing took place. A large hollow in the lower trunk was once used as a fuel store by the inn's landlord and visitors to Meavy in 1834 were assured that this cavity had once been used to host a dinner party for nine people.

The Meavy Oak and the Royal Oak Inn today.

The artist John White Abbott's depiction of the oak in 1831.

The village green, inn, and the Meavy Oak c.1930.

The suggestion that Meavy's original granite cross was set at the foot of the tree in order to 'Christianise' the site is not entirely implausible. But that cross went missing (see the section on Manaton), leaving behind just the socket stone, until it was discovered (minus its head and arms) in a nearby field serving as a gatepost. In the late 1800s a new head was set upon the original shaft.

The fifteenth-century Royal Oak Inn is an interesting gem among Dartmoor's hostelries, not least as it is owned by the parish council with profits going to the community. It was originally one of many Church House inns on the moor.

SHEEPSTOR

The village and church lie in the shadow of Sheepstor.

The author Philip Weller places Sheepstor as being a possible location for Baskerville Hall, although for the imaginary Hall itself he suggests candidates farther afield. In support of his theory he points to references in *The Hound*:

> ...such as the fact that there is a track leading from 'Baskerville Hall' directly across the Moor for nine miles to the farm of the yeoman whose daughter was abducted by the wicked Hugo Baskerville... Given that 'Baskerville Hall' lay on the East-South-Eastern rim of the Moor, and the distance involved, the suggestion is that this track must have run towards somewhere on the South-Western rim of the Moor, with the village of Sheepstor being a good candidate...

The wicked Hugo Baskerville pursued across the moor by the hound.

A possible candidate for the fictional Baskerville Hall? Burrator House as it looked in the early 1900s. The Rajah of Sarawak came to live here in 1863 and is buried in Sheepstor churchyard.

99

The now ruined Longstone Manor near Sheepstor. "In the fading light I could see that the centre was a heavy block of building from which a porch projected." Dr Watson on first seeing Baskerville Hall.

Philip Weller suggests Sheepstor as a possible location of Baskerville Hall. This rare image discovered in the Dartmoor Trust Archive reveals a number of similarities to the remains of Longstone Manor seen above. Is this the original Baskerville Hall?

In fact there exists at least one candidate for the Hall itself, that being Burrator House, former home of Sir James Brooke, the Rajah of Sarawak, to which he retired in 1868. An early photograph, the house looking suitably dramatic, suggests it would make an ideal candidate for Baskerville Hall, at least for film or television use.

However, perhaps a better candidate has come to light since Weller published *Hunting the Dartmoor Legend*, a building which fits the seventeenth century origins of Baskerville Hall – and conforms to Doyle's description:

> *In the fading light I could see that the centre was a heavy block of building from which a porch projected. The whole front was draped in ivy, with a patch clipped bare here and there where a window or a coat-of-arms broke through the dark veil.*

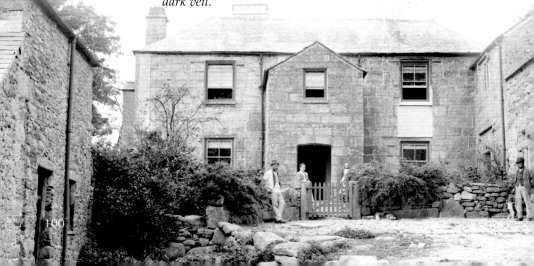

In researching the book *Dartmoor Century II*, published to celebrate the work of the Dartmoor Trust Archive, a then unidentified photograph of an early Dartmoor building came to light which has subsequently been closely matched to the ruins of Longstone Manor at Sheepstor, home to the ancient Elford family – themselves of legendary note.

Park Cottage Inn at Burrator, closed in the early 1900s.

Longstone Manor was forcibly abandoned at around the time Doyle came to Dartmoor due to its location at the edge of Burrator Reservoir, then under construction. Its eerie ruins, now a protected monument, stand at the very edge of the reservoir.

The inn at Burrator, the Park Cottage Inn, closed in the early decades of the 1900s after enjoying a period of boom while the reservoir was under construction. The landlord was then Joseph Nelder, while earlier, in the 1890s, one Charles Mortimer was recorded here as a 'beer retailer'. There is no inn today at Sheepstor, the nearest being the Royal Oak at Meavy and the Burrator Inn at Dousland (originally called the Manor Hotel).

ROBOROUGH

When the twenty-three year old Doyle set out on his excursion from Plymouth to Tavistock in 1882, the outlying settlements, some now incorporated into the urban sprawl of the city, were very much separate and distinct. Roborough, Yelverton, Horrabridge and Whitchurch, each

The Lopes Arms is the ivy-covered building halfway along the street, disguised as the Admiral Vernon by Doyle in his 1882 trip to Dartmoor.

remained largely untouched by the march of time despite the railway encircling the moor's western edge. Even twenty years later, at the time Doyle visits Princetown in 1901, Black's *Guide to Devonshire* warns would-be travellers:

> *A drawback to Dartmoor is the want of accommodation and shops which must be sought rather in the towns lying around its edge... ways over the centre are for the most part mere tracks, which must be followed with care, special heed being given to perilous patches of bog that might swallow up an unwary traveller, horse and man.*

Whether such perils were in the mind of the author and his two companions we will never know but they clearly found even the main roads wearying for after a few miles Doyle writes:

The track over Roborough Down at the end of the 1800s.

> *The long summer evening was drawing to a close before we trudged into the pretty little village of Roborough, where we had determined to put up for the night. The old English inn — with its signpost of Admiral Vernon and a kitchen door left artfully open to waft a savoury odour into the street — was so irresistible that I was fortunate we had pre-arranged to make it our head-quarters.*

It appears the author fictionalised the name of the inn, a trait throughout his writing as we have seen in *The Hound*. Thus the Lopes Arms appears to be the best candidate for their overnight stay, a seventeenth century former coaching house to which the Baskerville horse bus ran from Plymouth.

SHAUGH PRIOR

The hellish Wisht Hounds of Wistman's Wood reappear here at Shaugh Prior where we again find a possible inspiration for the Baskerville hound. Unlike the tales of solitary Black Shuck, many Dartmoor stories are associated with packs of hounds. Such legends are to be found at Hound Tor, Wistman's Wood, Bowerman's Nose and here, in the shadow of the Dewerstone, the 'Devil's Stone'. These packs of hound are derived from earlier mythologies, such as those connected with Thor, and in Britain are the creatures with which Satan himself hunts human souls. In *The Hound* the good Hugo Baskerville concludes his account of the Baskerville legend by warning that his sons *"...should forebear from crossing the moor in those dark hours when the powers of evil are exalted."*

The Dewerstone depicted in an early engraving.

Moonlight bathes the Dewerstone in ghastly light. Here the Devil would chase travellers to the highest crag leaving them to fall to their deaths straight into the waiting jaws of his spectral hounds below.

Doyle includes the Dewerstone in his short story 'The Winning Shot', published in 1882, which is set on the western moor.

Above us towered two great columns of rock, between which the water trickled to form a deep, still pool at the bottom.

The White Thorn Inn was built in the 1930s, replacing an earlier inn, now a cottage that stands nearby.

A perfect description of this remarkable natural feature which stands overlooking the River Plym around half a mile from the village of Shaugh Prior.

The present White Thorn Inn, built in the 1930s, replaces the earlier inn here that is now converted as a cottage.

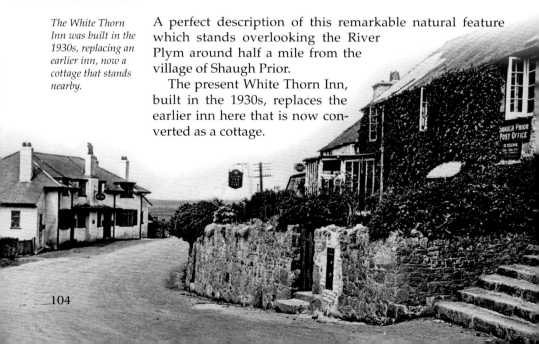

THE SOUTHERN MOOR

SPARKWELL

The A38 Devon Expressway from Exeter to Plymouth forms much of the southern boundary of the Dartmoor National Park. The old A38 meanders alongside the newer road passing through all the towns and villages that once provided accommodation for travellers. Sadly, many of the coaching houses, inns and hotels have disappeared, being demolished or converted into dwellings.

Had Doyle been in need of more large country houses on which to construct the imaginary Baskerville Hall, he would have found no shortage in this area. From the end of the eighteenth century wealthy Plymouth merchants, mine owners and those who had grown rich on woollen mills, chose to move out to the edge of the moor where land was plentiful and the air was clean.

Though the site is much older, the present Beechwood House was completed in 1802 by the Rosdew family. The Treby family, lawyers and politicians, were also among the most influential of the local squirearchy. They owned much land hereabouts and their name is perpetuated today in the Treby Arms.

Sir Henry and Dr Watson arrive at Baskerville Hall. Sydney Paget's original illustration.

Beechwood House, a plausible stand-in for Baskerville Hall?

Taken a hundred years apart, these photographs show little has changed at the Treby Arms, except the food.

DECANTING MACHINE.

Invaluable for Crusted Wines, Burgundy Baskets, &c.

Complete
Catalogues,
Post
Free.

To survive today pubs have to provide more than warm beer and a cosy place to sit. Along with others the Treby Arms has entered the field of fine dining and has earned a reputation as one of the best eating places in the county. This belies the building's more humble origins, built at the end of a row of eighteenth century cottages with a wheelwright's workshop attached.

CORNWOOD

Cornwood lies at the edge of Dartmoor where the ancient moorland road dribbles its way into the heart of the western moor. The parish offers a number of possible inspirations for Baskerville Hall in the shape of Blatchford, Slade and Delamore, fine country houses that each, in their own way, measure up to Doyle's imagined retreat.

It is almost certain that the author of *The Hound*, on his train journeys to and from Plymouth while working as a doctor, would have caught glimpses of these stately piles from the heights of Brunel's Slade viaduct on the Great Western line.

Brunel's Slade viaduct, built in 1849, is one of three in a short stretch of line running past Cornwood.

The Raleigh family had connections to nearby Fardel manor, and legends persist that Elizabeth Throckmorton, wife of Sir Walter Raleigh, retired to Cornwood after his execution carrying the family treasure which she buried here. Known as the Dark Lady, for she wears a dress of black silk, her ghost is said to haunt the lanes hereabouts. More disturbingly, in life she is said to have carried her husband's shrivelled head with her in a leather bag!

Slade House, from a drawing of 1894, is another home that fits Dr Watson's description of his first view of Baskerville Hall: "In the fading light I could see that the centre was a heavy block of building from which a porch projected. The whole front was draped in ivy, with a patch clipped bare here and there."

In the 1850s the inns recorded in the locality were the Tavistock Inn, the Butchers Arms (Moor Cross), the Cornwood Inn and the Mountain Inn (Lutton). Of these only the Cornwood Inn survives, although locals are calling for support to restore the Mountain Inn as a going concern.

The Cornwood Inn c.1910 and today. It is the only surviving inn here.

Elizabeth Throck-morton, the Dark Lady of Cornwood.

IVYBRIDGE

The Ivy Bridge with the White Swan on the right.

Ivybridge, as with its neighbours which stood along the old coaching route in and out of the westcountry, was once awash with inns, hotels, and beerhouses. In *White's Directory* of 1850 fifteen are listed as being in the Ivybridge district, including the Albert, the Bridge, the Erme, the George, the Grocers Arms, the Imperial, the Duke of Cornwall, the White Horse and the London Inn. At the coming of the railway a number of new hotels sprang up, offering more luxurious accommodation than many of the traditional inns.

The earliest known written reference to an inn here appears in an indenture dated 1672 which records that Alexander Pearse then held a ten years' lease on the 'Three Tonns'. An early depiction of an inn appears in a print of the original 'Ivy Bridge', dating from 1790, showing the inn sign of The Swan which later became the London Hotel.

This latter hostelry was built around the end of the eighteenth century and it rapidly became a principal inn as improved roads brought more coaching parties to the area.

In June 1848, following the completion of Brunel's magnificent Ivybridge viaduct, the South Devon Railway opened their station here bringing more visitors and described in Black's *Guide to Devonshire* of 1898 as providing 'one of the favourite railways excursions out of Plymouth'.

It is perhaps this close attachment to the railway that Philip Weller surmises that it was at Ivybridge station that Inspector Lestrade alighted having arrived from London to help in the arrest of Jack Stapleton at the request of Sherlock Holmes.

The area's other connection to *The Hound* is the use of nearby Lukesland, a Victorian Gothic pile built in 1862 which featured as Baskerville Hall in the 1968 BBC production of *The Hound of the Baskervilles* starring Peter Cushing as Sherlock Holmes.

The London Hotel was once Ivybridge's most popular hostelry, enjoying its heyday in the mid to late 1800s. By the mid 1900s it was in decline and finally closed in 1991.

Spanning the valley approaching Ivybridge station, this early photograph shows Brunel's original viaduct in place. It was replaced by a new stone structure in the 1890s.

Ivybridge: the Kings Arms, formerly the Fighting Cocks, now The Exchange. Below: Duke of Cornwall, 1920s and today

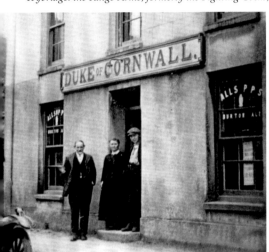

Below: The White Horse, Fore Street Ivybridge in the 1940s and today, renamed the Old Smithy.

SOUTH BRENT

South Brent lies beneath the shadow of the distinctive Brent Hill which rises to 300 metres a little north-east. Its location owes much to the fledgling River Avon as it flows off the high moor, well-placed for water to power its mills associated with the woollen trade. This thriving industry supported a healthy number of inns and in 1850 five are listed, despite a total population of little more than a thousand souls. Today the population is rising in all the villages that at first struggled after the new A38 bypassed them. They have now become desirable places to live, charming and quiet and yet within easy commuter reach of the cities. South Brent is doubly fortunate in that it has managed to hold on to most of its historic inns.

There is much to be made of the area with regard to *The Hound of the Baskervilles* both through notional locations and through speculating on the narrative elements as characters travel to and from the moor.

In *Hunting the Dartmoor Legend*, for instance, Philip Weller suggests South Brent as being an outside candidate for the station at which Dr Watson, Sir Henry and James Mortimer arrive from London. As Doyle describes it:

The train pulled up at a small wayside station and we all descended. Outside, beyond the low, white fence, a wagonette with a pair of cobs was waiting. Our coming was evidently a great event, for station-master and porters clustered round us to carry out our luggage. It was a sweet, simple country spot...

South Brent (or Brent) station as it appeared in the early 1900s.

113

The Anchor Hotel c.1910 and today.

If the supposition is correct that the better candidates for houses on which Doyle based Baskerville Hall lie in the southern reaches of the moor, then other locations mentioned in *The Hound of the Baskervilles* are easier to place. Among Doyleian scholars much conjecture for instance has been given to the location of Black Tor, on the summit of which Dr Watson spies the mysterious lone figure:

God help those who wander into the Great Mire now, for even the firm uplands are becoming a morass. I found the Black Tor upon which I had seen the solitary watcher, and from its craggy summit... in the distant hollow on the left, half hidden by the mist, the two thin towers of Baskerville Hall.

There are at least three tors so named on Dartmoor but Philip Weller puts his money firmly on the Black Tor which stands above the River Aune, a mile or so north of South Brent over-looking Shipley Bridge. This area would also fit with Dr Mortimer's archaeological work and the description of the prehistoric stone hut in which Sherlock Holmes secreted himself, for Brent Moor abounds with such remains.

Sydney Paget's original illustration of the 'solitary watcher' on Black Tor.

Above: The Royal Oak c.1930 and The Oak today. Below: The Pack Horse early 1900s and today.

113

The tomb of wicked Richard Cabell stands among the gravestones in Buckfastleigh churchyard.

BUCKFASTLEIGH

Before the south porch is the enclosed tomb of Richard Cabell of Brook, who died in 1677. He was the last male of his race, and died with such an evil reputation that he was placed under a heavy stone, and a sort of penthouse was built over that with iron gratings to it, to prevent his coming up and haunting the neighbourhood. When he died, the story goes that fiends and black dogs breathing fire raced over Dartmoor and surrounded Brook, howling.

Revd Sabine Baring-Gould, *Devonshire*

The shell of Buckfastleigh church is all that remains following the fire in 1992.

Buckfastleigh lies at the heart of the story of *The Hound of the Baskervilles* for, it is said, it was the legend of the wicked Squire Cabell that drew Doyle to set his tale on Dartmoor. Fletcher Robinson, Doyle's colleague (some say collaborator), almost certainly knew of the legend as he was brought up in Ipplepen a mere eight miles from Cabell's last resting place.

In fact there are a number of legends connecting Cabell to devilish goings-on in the area and to the appearance of spectral black dogs associated with this death. The real-life Richard Cabell was the third so named of that family to live

Brook Manor, now a private residence with no public access, was Richard Cabell's family home and thought to be a possible location for Baskerville Hall.

on Dartmoor. A local squire, he lived at Brook Manor, a few miles to the north of Buckfastleigh. He was extremely unpopular in the neighbourhood, being known as 'Dirty Dick', leading a dissolute life; a wife killer suspected of indulging in the black arts.

The story lives on locally in the shape of the Cabell family tomb which sits foursquare among the common gravestones in Buckfastleigh's Holy Trinity churchyard. The church itself is now but a shell, having been gutted by fire as the result of arson in 1992. And superstition surrounds the tomb itself for children were dared to put their finger in the keyhole of the tomb's lock on pain of the Devil biting it!

The wealth of this area was built on wool and the making of cloth, and a further legend concerns the ghost of a weaver who lived nearby at Deancombe. Unquiet, the weaver's spirit sat at its ghostly loom until a priest threw a handful of soil from the churchyard at the ghost which immediately turned into a black hound. The hound was given the task of emptying a pool in the adjacent Dean Burn, using a nutshell with a hole in it, and the pool has ever since been known as Hound Pool.

Since the first publication of The Hound of the Baskervilles *in 1901, artists and filmakers have interpreted their personal vision of the hound. Here, sculptor Mairi Laing has depicted the massive creature standing alongside Fox Tor Mire Cross on Dartmoor.*

Buckfastliegh railway station c.1900, viewed from Dartbridge Road.

A branch line from Totnes once passed through Buck-fastleigh and ran on to Ashburton and is the Doyleian scholar's first choice for the 'wayside station' described in *The Hound* at which Dr Watson and his party alight before making their way to Baskerville Hall. It certainly would offer relatively easy access to the moor via one of the many lanes wandering vaguely northwards.

Following the closure of the line it was taken over for preservation by the Dart Valley Light Railway with the first train running between Buckfastleigh and Totnes in 1969. This provides a welcome focus for visitors to the area.

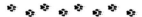

The Valiant Soldier, a pub frozen in time.

Strangely, among the best known inns in Buckfastleigh is one where no drinks are served. This is the Valiant Soldier, closed in the late 1960s after which, for thirty years, it remained

practically untouched with the bars and everything in them providing a fascinating time capsule. Purchased in 1997 by the local authority and held in trust, it is now a museum.

At the time of Doyle's visit to Dartmoor there were eight public houses listed in Buckfastleigh including the White Hart, the Valiant Soldier, the Half Moon, the Globe, the Mechanics Arms, the Royal Oak, the Golden Lion, the Town Arms and the Watermans Arms. Of these the Globe, the White Hart and the Kings Arms remain in the centre of the town.

The Waterman Arms Buckfastleigh, named after the Waterman family who ran it. This photograph, taken around the time The Hound *was first published, gives an idea of the road surfaces and difficulties of travel on and around Dartmoor at that period.*

The Globe today.

Above: The Kings Arms Buckfastleigh, 1930s and today.

HOLNE

The Church House Inn at Holne has claims to be one of the oldest in Devon. Robert Burnard, Dartmoor antiquarian and pioneer photographer, in his book *Dartmoor Pictorial Records*, records that the incumbent vicar of Holne (c.1890) "believes that this is the existing Church House or 'Tavistock Inn', which building would then date back to 1329."

It has been suggested that at one time there was a Church House in every parish in Devon and of those that survive there are at least a dozen on Dartmoor. Despite their name, these buildings were outside the control of the church and were very much in the hands of the local people, being used specifically for community activities. Traditionally ale was brewed here and gatherings and celebrations of various kinds took place. They were thus a combination of village hall and local inn.

The Church House Inn today and as photographed by Robert Burnard in 1889.

Cleft Rock as photographed by Robert Burnard in January 1891 provides a possible location for Doyle's 'Cleft Tor' in The Hound of the Baskervilles. *It is no longer possible to visit the site for it is on private property and, moreover, is dangerously over-grown.*

Philip Weller puts forward the former Holne Chase Hotel, originally built as a private residence, as being a possible candidate for Baskerville Hall.

Along with the Church House, Robert Burnard also photographed the nearby feature 'Cleft Rock' which some have suggested fits the description of Doyle's 'Cleft Tor' from which Sir Henry Baskerville and Dr Watson observe a tiny point of yellow light shining 'a mile or two' distant from Baskerville Hall, assuming it to be the lair of the hound.

IPPLEPEN

Although somewhat outside the moorland boundary, the little village of Ipplepen plays a significant part in the story of *The Hound of the Baskervilles*, for this place was the family home – and final resting place – of Doyle's great friend Bertram Fletcher Robinson.

Much debate has surrounded Fletcher Robinson's role in the writing of *The Hound* but suffice to say that authors draw on many sources for the inspiration behind their writings, and Doyle was no exception.

What we do know is that, during his visit to Dartmoor in 1901, Doyle wrote to his mother from the Duchy Hotel in Princetown to say 'Tomorrow we drive 16 miles to Ipplepen where R's parents live.' Their destination was Fletcher Robinson's parent's home Park Hill House, a substantial Victorian

Bertram Fletcher Robinson's grave in Ipplepen churchyard.

Park Hill House in Ipplepen. On the left is Park Hill Lodge that was formerly the carriage house from which Harry Baskerville departed to drive Fletcher Robinson and Doyle across Dartmoor.

Arthur Conan Doyle, young cricketer.

residence built around 1850 for a local cider merchant, John Bowden. The house was later purchased by Joseph Fletcher Robinson, Bertram's father, whose carriage driver was Henry (known as Harry) Baskerville. Both Harry and Bertram had played cricket for Ipplepen and, of course, Doyle had been a keen cricketer from his youth, later playing for the MCC and claiming the scalp (his only in the first-class game) of the world's most famous batsman, W.G. Grace.

Legend has it that Sherlock was named as a combination of two Nottinghamshire cricketers, Sherwin and Shacklock. Shacklock later played for Derbyshire where his fellow fast bowler was William Mycroft, after whom Doyle named the brother of Sherlock (Mycroft Holmes).

At the time of their visit Fletcher Robinson and Doyle had the choice of two inns in the village, the Plough (landlord John Smith) and the Wellington Inn (landlord Samuel Easterbrook). The Plough closed in 2009.

Ipplepen photographed at around the period when Doyle visited in 1901. The Plough Inn (now closed) is on the left.

ASHBURTON

Ashburton Market Place c.1820. The Rose & Crown inn stands on the left of the market house.

Ashburton was once a town of pubs. In 1850 sixteen inns are listed, all clustered close to the centre of the town, but occasional beerhouses brought the overall number of drinking places nearer to thirty. At the time Arthur Conan Doyle came to Dartmoor around thirteen of these remained and, three years later, the 1904 Licensing Act came into force:

North Street early 1900s, the Town Arms distant right.

...to deal with that unbridled indulgence in alcohol, that habitual tippling and drunkenness, which are playing such havoc with our civilisation. The magnitude of the evil is undeniable; its results are patent in every direction, in every class; while the ravages of the scourge are even more terrible among women than among men.

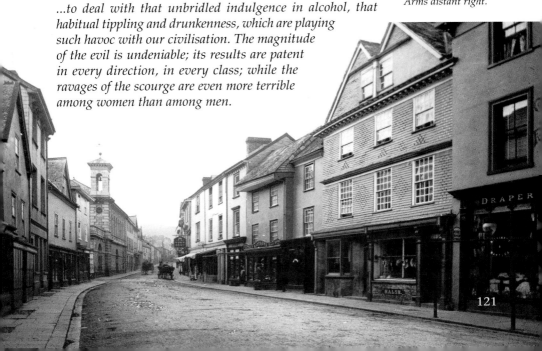

121

Decorating the Bull Ring for Queen Victoria's Jubilee, the Sun Inn behind.

The sites of at least four existing and former pubs can be seen in this photo, the Mermaid Inn and Town Arms on the right and the Commercial Inn and the Globe on the left.

Under the Act beerhouses that closed were compensated, the funds being provided by a levy on the owners of the premises, usually the brewers). In Ashburton this led to a licensing review, with the authorities expressing concern over seven licensed houses that stood within 20 yards of each other. Consequently several were closed, part of the decline in the number of pubs throughout England from 1904 onwards.

The town appears to have a propensity for alcohol and in the eighteenth century gave its name to a drink known as Ashburton Pop, described here by John Cooke who was born at the Rose and Crown in Ashburton in 1765:

Earlier called the First and Last, the Victoria Inn in North Street was, in the eighteenth century, a terrace of weavers' cottages.

This town has been famous for a beverage called Ashburton Pop as London is for porter. I recollect its sharp feeling good taste, far richer than the best small beer, more of the champaign taste, and what was termed a good sharp bottle, when you untied and hand-drew the cork, it gave a report louder than a pop-gun, to which I attribute its name: its contents would fly up to the ceiling if you did not mind to keep the mouth of the bottle into the white quart cup, it filled it with froth, but not over a pint of clear liquor. Three old cronies would sit an afternoon, six hours, smoke, and drink a dozen bottles, their reckoning but eight pence each and a penny for tobacco. The pop was but tuppence a bottle. It's a great novel loss to the town, because its recipe died with its brewers about 1785.

The Bay Horse is a relative latecomer to Ashburton. It was earlier called the Barnstaple Inn and served men using the old packhorse route between Barnstaple and Brixham. It is possibly one of the two North Street beerhouses mentioned in the 1850 directories.

West Street and The Exeter Inn in 1897 and today. Below: The Golden Lion Hotel c. 1930 and as residential flats today.

Below: East Street and the Royal Oak in the 1930s and as it is today.

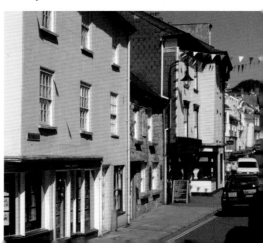

Listed in 1850 as the Old Bottle, the inn became the Railway Hotel in 1872 serving the South Devon branch line from Totnes. It took the name Silent Whistle in the 1960s after the line closed.

Ashburton also keeps up the practice of Ale Tasting, once an important civic duty ensuring the quality of ale made and sold in the town was kept up to acceptable standard. Having died out for some years the ceremony was revived in 1943, though now more fun than function.

But there was also dissent against drinking, for in 1880 the *Western Morning News* reported:

> *The Sunday Closing Association had recently sent representatives to advocate stopping the sale of alcohol on Sundays. As a result of a meeting at the Market Hall Messrs Craddock, Down, Clark and Mann had distributed and collected voting papers to Ashburton householders. Of the 75% who responded, 203 voted for closing, 53 had voted against, and 42 had no preference either way.*

Ashburton's legend revolves around the startling behaviour of a figure known as 'Cutty Dyer' who haunted the River Yeo, abducting children and terrorizing drunks. Like Doyle's hound he is described as having blazing eyes as large as saucers. It's probable, as with other hound legends associated with the moor, the origins of this frightful apparition are the folk memories of all that remain of much older myths.

Ashburton's enduring connection to *The Hound of the Baskervilles* rests on the lifestory of Henry (Harry) Baskerville, the coachman who took Arthur Conan Doyle and his friend Bertram Fletcher Robinson on their fateful trip to Princetown in 1901. Harry had already worked for the Robinson family for fifteen years when he was charged with taking the party out to Princetown, thus he and Bertram would have been well acquainted.

Harry was thirty when he first met Doyle who was a dozen years his senior. Harry's schooling ended when he was eleven and in the strict social code of those times, Harry would have observed the necessary deference to his passengers – although Doyle's purpose for visiting the moor to get background 'colour' for his story, and his naturally inquisitive and sociable manner, would have broken down those barriers to a degree.

In 1907 Harry left the employ of the Robinson family but by then would have spent some years basking in the reflected glory of what had become a world famous story. At this time he moved from Ipplepen to take up work with Ashburton businessman, John Sawdye, who owned the London Inn and, later, the Golden Lion. Here, by all accounts, he became a popular member of the community living at 'Dorncliffe', a modest house in West Street until his death in 1962.

During his later life Harry was interviewed on numerous occasions by journalists and writers who sought his views and, as with many good stories, Harry's tales

Harry Baskerville ended his working life in the employ of John Sawdye who owned the Golden Lion in Ashburton. Here we see the hotel in its heyday c.1905.

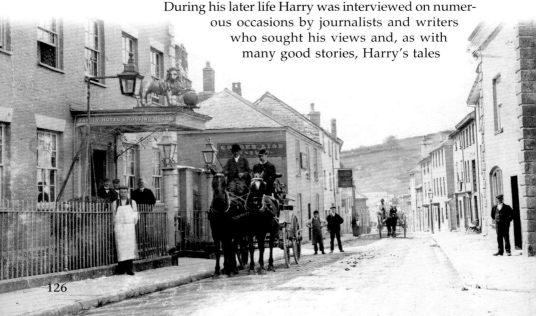

became embellished over time, providing those who would believe them with their own opportunities to speculate and sensationalise the inspirations behind the writing of *The Hound*, and even on who actually wrote it. As Philip Weller has written 'Harry's suggestions have been revived at regular intervals, as new generations of commentators have "rediscovered" the controversy.' Intrigue and mystery has literally dogged the footsteps of Doyle's original characters creating a new industry that continues to this day to attract writers and film makers.

This book primarily intends only to draw on the story of *The Hound* to encourage visitors to Dartmoor to discover for themselves some of the places associated with it, and with the moor's own enduring legends. If it has a serious purpose it is to draw attention to the importance of preserving historical photographs and, in a small way, to support rural inns that are increasingly under threat.

Ashburton churchyard. Harry Baskerville's gravestone commemorating his life and that of his wife, Alice.

BIBLIOGRAPHY

Baring-Gould, S. *Devonshire*, Methuen & Co., 1907.

Beard, Hillary. *Buckfast in Bygone Days*, Devon Books, 1991.

Bellamy, Reg. *The Book of Postbridge*, Devon Books, 1998.

Brewer, Dave. *Dartmoor Boundary Markers*, Devon Books, 2002.

Brown, Theo. *Devon Ghosts*, Jarrold, 1982.

Butler, Simon (ed.). *A Gentleman's Walking Tour of Dartmoor*, Devon Books, 1986.

Butler, Simon. *Dartmoor Century*, Halsgrove, 2000.

Butler, Simon. *Dartmoor Century II*, Halsgrove, 2001.

Butler, Simon. *The Farmer's Wife*, Halsgrove, 2013.

Butler, Simon. *Goodbye Old Friend*, Halsgrove, 2012.

Dart, Maurice. *Plymouth & South Devon Railways*, Halsgrove, 2007.

Dobinson, M. et al. *The Book of Cornwood and Lutton*, Halsgrove, 1997.

Coleman, Sandra. *The Book of Buckfastleigh*, Halsgrove, 2003

Crossing, W. *Crossing's Guide to Dartmoor*, Peninsula Press, 1990.

Crossing, W. *Gems in a Granite Setting*, Western Morning News, 1905.

Crossing, W. *One Hundred Years on Dartmoor*, Western Morning News, 1901.

Doyle, Arthur Conan. 'Dry Plates on a Dry Moor', *British Journal of Photography*, 1882.

Doyle, Arthur Conan. *The Hound of the Baskervilles.* George Newnes Ltd, 1902.

Gardner-Thorpe, C. *The Book of Princetown*, Halsgrove, 2003

Gover, J.E.B. et al. *The Place Names of Devon*, 2 Vols. Cambridge U.P. 1973.

Harrison, Bill. *Dartmoor Stone Crosses*, Devon Books, 2001.

Hemery, Eric. *High Dartmoor*, Robert Hale, 1983.

Hemery, Pauline. *The Book of Meavy*, Halsgrove, 1999.

Le Messurier, Brian. *Dartmoor Artists*, Halsgrove, 2002

Martin, Ivor. *The Book of Ivybridge*, Halsgrove, 2009.

Mercer, Ian. *Dartmoor,* Collins New Naturalist Library, 2010.

Moncrieff, A.R. Hope. *Black's Guide to Devonshire*, A&C Black, 1898.

Pugh, Brian et al. *Arthur Conan Doyle, Sherlock Holmes and Devon*, MX Publishing, 2010.

Phillpotts, Eden. *My Devon Year*, MacMillan, 1903

Quick, Tom. *Dartmoor Inns*, Devon Books, 1992.

Radford, U. and R. *The Book of South Tawton and South Zeal*, Halsgrove, 2000.

Rice, Iain. *The Book of Chagford*, Halsgrove, 2002.

Stanbrook, Elisabeth. *Dartmoor Forest Farms*, Devon Books, 1994.

Tregoning, Lance. *Bovey Tracey in Bygone Days*, Devon Books,1989.

Hands, S. and Webb, P. *The Book of Ashburton*, Halsgrove, 2012.

Wall, Greg. *The Book of South Brent*, Halsgrove

Weller, P.. *The Hound of the Baskervilles. Hunting the Dartmoor Legend*, Devon Books, 2001.

Woodcock, G. *The Book of Tavistock*, Halsgrove, 2003.

Woods, Stephen. *Dartmoor Farm*, Halsgrove, 2003.

Woods, Stephen. *The Book of Widecombe*, Devon Books, 1996.

Wyatt, Monica. *Historic Inns of Devon*, Bossiney Books, 1986.